The International Design Yearbook
1998

Editor – Richard Sapper
General Editor – Michael Horsham
Assistant Editor – Jennifer Hudson
Art Direction/Design – Tomato

Abbeville Press   Publishers
New York   London   Paris

First published in the United States of America in 1998 by Abbeville Press,
22 Cortlandt Street, New York, NY 10007

First published in Great Britain in 1998 by Laurence King Publishing
an imprint of Calmann & King Ltd
71 Great Russell Street
London WC1B 3BN

Copyright © 1998 Calmann & King Ltd

ISBN 0-7892-0375-8

First edition
10 9 8 7 6 5 4 3 2 1

Based on an original idea by Stuart Durant
Printed in Hong Kong

Contents

The International Design Yearbook
1998

Introductions

In the foreword to last year's edition Philippe Starck wrote about the need for an evolutionary progress of design as opposed to frantic revolutions. I imagine he was referring to the several waves of fashionable styles which we have endured in the past ten or twenty years — and which have certainly not contributed to making the objects of our daily life more interesting. One only has to try to distinguish the makes of the cars passing by on the street to see examples of this. However, while these movements have been completely superficial and have originated either in some passing intellectual trend or in marketing strategies connected to planned obsolescence — which it is difficult to distinguish from common fraud — there can be little doubt that in socio-economic and technological terms we are living not in an evolutionary period but in one of the most violent revolutions of the last thousand years.

I am not thinking here of the industrial revolution, the Communist revolution or the two World Wars, but of things that have happened in the last ten years and will happen in the next ten years. It is a sort of peaceful revolution, and many people, including most politicians, have not even realized that it exists, but it does. Product designers, especially if they work for big, technological companies, have a very good overview of what will hit the streets in the next five years, and what is happening in factories now, so some comment from me might be justified.

Consider these technical developments: in the last twenty years the subminiaturization of computing technology has reduced the volume of a given measure of computing capacity by a factor of one thousand, and this reduction does not show any sign of changing course. This means that what filled a computer room (at a cost proportionate to its size) twenty years ago will fit into the sole of your shoe ten years from now (still at a cost proportionate to its size). As a result, every human activity based on routine and repetition will be economically reproducible by a robot, even playing chess against a reasonably good player. New developments make it possible to print computer chips (or an electric motor) on paper substrates, which means that a newspaper could become a computer, connected by radio (incorporated) and satellite to the whole globe. Distances will become completely irrelevant (even today the trip from Milan to Heathrow is quicker than that from Heathrow to the British Museum), and the globalization of economy will become total. This means that any difference in living standards between different regions will be abolished, and that it will no longer be possible to determine national tax policies (even today production and employment are moving to countries with lower taxes). All these things, which will reorganize the lives and existence of us all and of our children in a technical and socio-economic way, are only one side of this revolution, however. The other is cultural. Will the effect of these developments, which are currently taking place at full speed, be to replace real life with one lived through the computer screen? Already there are aeroplanes on the drawing board without windows: what do you have to see the world? You have our entertainment programme. You want to go skiing? Here is our simulator.

Fortunately, real life will not in all probability be substituted by virtual reality because every movement creates reaction, and these developments may heighten our awareness of other fields and materials. I do not think that our future world will be entirely without material objects, but it may have fewer than we deem indispensable today. What is going to be important, what is going to be developed, depends on what is important to us, and what we are prepared to fight for.

With respect to scientific development, I am often reminded of Dave Barry's recent comment in the **International Herald Tribune**, relating to the impractical design of many of our everyday household items: '... and what is the scientific community doing about these problems? They're cloning sheep. Great! Just what we need! Sheep that look MORE ALIKE than they already do!' He could not be more right. Every time I watch television commercials I ask myself if they have ever shown me something I really need. Is there something I really need? Yes! An apple that tastes like those I stole as a kid (or last year along a country road in the Czech Republic), or a grapefruit like those my grandmother had (and which I luckily found again on Hollywood's Farmers Market), or a car that runs on hydrogen, or household electricity from sunlight and wind, or something else that gives me an emotion or a recollection of a beautiful memory, or serves a useful purpose, or feeds my imagination, or saves me something precious, or stuns me with surprise at a really new idea.

These are things we need, and some of them can be created by a designer – I hope that you might even find some in this book – but they are not only created by designers; they could be made by an engineer, a farmer, a child, by anyone, but above all they are brought to us by the entrepreneur.

When I studied economical sciences at Munich University, one of the dogmas I learnt was that profit is the reward for a service rendered to society. This dogma, it seems to me, has not made it into these times of the CEO, stockholders' equity, next quarterly results and the Harvard Business School. I think that it is an interesting phenomenon that the French word entrepreneur (**Unternehmer** in German, **Imprenditore** in Italian etc) does not exist in English. This most important figure of Western capitalism does not exist in English! Well, naturally he exists, but he has no name, he hides himself! He has become a CEO. But he is the guy who has to render the service to society, and he should be able to distribute a dividend to his shareholders only according to the degree in which this service has been rendered. The same naturally applies to our elected politicians. So what do you think of the budget deficit which says in clear terms: let our children pay for the debts we make? What of the impossibility of raising an energy tax which would make it impractical to burn fossil fuels and could finance reproducible energy sources, thereby helping them to develop the few steps more they need to make them competitive?

You say: what has this got to do with design? I think: everything. All design, but especially the design of our products, cannot be divided from our life – it has been like that since the dawn of time. What we design and what we produce is what we live with – but it is not necessarily what we need. Much of what we can buy today is useless junk (like cloned sheep) and many things we would need to make our lives better, and the future of our world better, we cannot get, because we do not shout for them, ask for them, fight for them, because we believe that those wonderful people up there on the television screen advertising this or that are so much more beautiful and happy than we are that they must be right.

It is a fact that life, which is mirrored by design, can only be changed by the imagination, the ideas and the will of people, individually or in groups, and that apathy is the most dangerous poison of society. So I want to make a most passionate plea: think about what you want in life, for you and for your children, what sort of a world you would want, and ask for it, loud and clearly, alone and with others. We live in an economy that listens to what people want, and we as designers regard it as our responsibility to create those things that can improve our life and our future. But we need the call from the public, if we don't get it, our CEO will tell us: I can make more money with cosmetics, or gene-manipulated corn, or cloned sheep or the Eurofighter – which as I have just learnt, costs three times as much as it did to build the Channel Tunnel.

Richard Sapper

Richard Sapper
Espresso Coffee Machine – Coban
cast aluminium
h 39cm – l 25.5cm – d 25.5cm
h 15 3/8in – l 10in – d 10in
Alessi – Italy – 1997

Richard Sapper
Stacking Chair – Aida
steel tube – polypropylene
h 85cm – l 52cm – d 56cm
h 33 1/2in – l 20 1/2in – d 22in
Magis – Italy – 1997

Richard Sapper
IBM Notebook Computer – Thinkpad 700C
designed with Kaz Yamazaki
1992

Richard Sapper
Digital Clock – Rocket
Italora – Italy – 1971

Richard Sapper
Radio – TS502 – designed with Marco Zanuso
Brionvega – 1963

Richard Sapper
Table Lamp – Tizio
Artemide – Italy – 1972

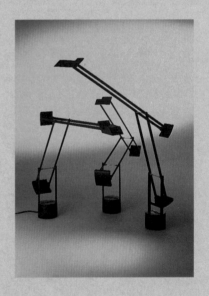

The things we choose to own and display in our homes, to a large extent, help us to define who we are. It doesn't matter if we are dealing with collectors of readymade limited edition 'artworks' – plates depicting anything from cute kittens in a basket to the oil-well fires of the Gulf War – or those who choose to furnish their homes with 'taste', 'authority' and 'aplomb' using the 'latest' designs from the 'latest' designers. Whichever the case, we are all – in the developed consumer economies, at least – users of the designed object as commodity. This fact leads us to a simple idea. That is that to choose, use and display an object is to enter into a system of commodity and communication.

Despite the undeniable presence of the communicative power of commodities, and our need to understand that power, it may be the case that as we spiral through our own personal late twentieth-century shopathons, certain thinkers and theoreticians who illuminate the process of acquisition and display have become less than prominent in the analyses of the ways, whys and wherefores of consumerism. Some, however, still offer us ways of thinking about ourselves in relation to things we choose to own.

Thorstein Veblen is one such thinker. Karl Marx another. Veblen famously identified the surfeit of labour inherent in luxury goods. In Marxist terms the concepts of use value and exchange value were identified as key when talking about the consumer object. A Marxist analysis of consumerism relates use value directly to an object's function – the felt hat to keep you warm; the knife to cut; the chair upon which to sit. The exchange value of a given object was, however, and still is a more difficult thing to pin down. Many elements combine and conspire to define an object's non-functional value and that value can and does change with time and context.

For example, why at present is the virtual pet – the tamagotchi – sought after at inflated prices? Answer: because its exchange value far exceeds its use – or even its monetary value. Costing a few pence to manufacture in the so-called tiger economies, and with no discernible functional value (other than the compulsive allure of the computer game), the tamagotchi is a representative example of the mystifying shifting power of exchange value.

This object has transcended its intended market position, its intended price, and even its intended function. It is no longer simply childish entertainment, but instead a status symbol. But then, everything is a status symbol. Exchange value? Go figure.

By the time this book reaches the shelves the tamagotchi phenomenon will have been superseded by some other nine-minute-wonder of our age. But the same principles will be governing the rise of the illuminated interactive spatula or whatever the next fad is, as have governed the tamagotchi's brief streak across the firmament of things-we-can-consume.

Marx did not have to deal with such solid state, mass market, pan-global hysteria. For those dealing with Marxist analyses, exchange value was closely allied to the amount of human work something took to make, together with the relationship of the worker to the work they were doing and the context in which the goods were consumed. By buying an expensive hand-wrought or worked item, the purchaser was in effect buying the time of the worker who had made the object. By implicating themselves in mass production, workers themselves ran the risk of alienation from the end result of their work. By selling their time and by tacitly acknowledging the exchange value of a given object the 'haves' and the 'have-nots' were glued together in a social DNA spiral of emulation and distinction.

Thus the exquisitely worked, handmade object carried almost by definition different values than its supposedly humbler or machine-made counterpart. In Marx's time, quality – in terms of the investment of human labour – was arguably easier to spot for the visually astute and aesthetically educated, if a tad more difficult to buy.

In our time, things may seem rather different on the surface, at least. We have robots making cars which look and feel as though they have been handmade. In our time, design for serial production has become the norm, and we are immune to the notion of rapidity of production as a negative idea. Yet objects still accrue status, value and price when they are worked upon for a long time by hand. For the majority of us, however, access to that world of value is either through the short-run work of the craftsperson or through the brand values of the couturier's diffusion and perfume line.

In our time, and importantly for the business of design, there are more of us in the world now and we all need things. On that basis, the object designed for mass production continues to hold sway, even if the idea of quality does not. All objects are designed by someone, somewhere. But not everyone everywhere is interested in the idea of quality. This may seem a simplistic truism but it highlights a further truth. That is, that there are responsibilities at the heart of the designer's job which may not seem apparent when glancing in the window in the high street.

Design for the domestic environment is shaped by the reflection of these responsibilities. The job of delivering objects which have the stamp of quality at their heart should never be far from a designer's mind when conceiving of a new product or re-rendering a domestic staple. Equally, the considerations of budgets, aesthetics, semantics and function should structure the approach to the product. Designers are, as we know, the orchestrators of compromises. Materials and their effects on the environment during the cradle to the grave existence of a product are also, we are told, increasingly at the forefront of designers' and manufacturers' concerns. The process of bringing together a book like this one reveals the extent to which the impetus to instill quality is often missing from the design process. But how do we recognize quality, and moreover quality in design? Is to design an object well to remove the element of human mark making which characterizes the process of making art and handworked objects? Given that the material expression of ourselves is open equally to invention and to interpretation, how do we identify the work which speaks to us of the mythical, and it has to be said, perhaps meaningless holy grail of 'good design'?

It would be a mistake to see this book as a manual pointing the way to the essence of good design. Rather, **The International Design Yearbook 1998** is a selection, as ever, of just some of the objects submitted for the scrutiny and ultimate sanction of the guest editor. This year the editor happens to be Richard Sapper, a man whose track record is undeniable in terms of innovation and commitment to the idea of producing designs that actually work. Chosen from thousands of submissions, the contents of the book reflect not so much the purely personal choices of a famous designer, as a selection from a vast and unmappable world of contemporary things. Not everything in the book can be judged to be excellent by all standards. Some objects will appeal to readers more than others; some will occasion disbelief; some envy. The multiplicity of approaches to the idea of design means that the book is a rich seam of examples from the contemporary culture of objects. That being the case, this book cannot help but in some way reflect the age.

In that sense, I believe that this book comes from a long tradition of mapping designers' approaches to the domestic. Perhaps stretching as far back as the work of Hermann Muthesius whose 1904–5 publication of **Das Englische Haus** focused upon the idea of the domestic as it was defined by English architects. Since the turn of the century, however, the definition of the domestic has shifted almost as much as the idea of design. Hence this book is far removed from the results achieved by Muthesius. Nevertheless the book represents at least one expression of a matrix of thought and deed surrounding the design of the domestic object, just as there is a matrix of thought and deed concerning what it means to live amongst the things we humans make.

The matrix is bounded by the ideas of material and meaning, and design and domesticity. By far the most engaging of these is the idea of domesticity. And today, the idea of the domestic is increasingly under scrutiny. It seems that culturally speaking, domesticity is 'in'. In popular culture, soap operas have turned the ordinary house interior into the location of dramatic narrative watched simultaneously by millions of people. In art, Rachel Whiteread has thrown the house interior into relief and objectified the idea of the home. By placing

Frogdesign
Macworld – Enterprise Power Mac
1996

Gerald Brandstatter
Cardboard Scooter
1997

Bär and Knell
12 Time Documents Chair
1996

Argelik
Direct Drive Washing Machine
1997

Nigel Coates
Legover Chair
1997

Michael Young
MY 025 – Fly Armchair
1996

Jasper Morrison
Atlas Table
1997

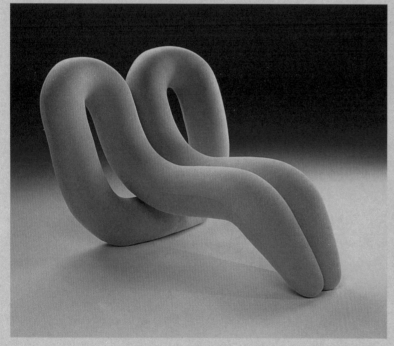

the inside on the outside, so to speak, Whiteread's 'House' and other works transform the usual locus of the private into the public. Equally, in photography the unflinching gaze of Nick Waplington or the stagey analysis of Martin Parr's imagery has revealed at least some of the preoccupations that cause people to choose the things with which they wish to live. Real lives are revealed to consist of little but the ownership of things and the striving for some sense of equilibrium.

Even fields that traditionally have concentrated upon the behaviours of 'others', the exotic, the uncivilized and the aboriginal, have found fascination in the behaviour of our deranged consumerist selves. This is true to the extent that anthropologists' field work can now include the behaviour of people on housing estates; their shopping patterns and the relationships they form with inanimate objects. That ordinary things are loaded with meaning and significance that their designers and their consumers could not conceive is as compelling an idea as it ever was. The ordinary has become truly and incontrovertibly extraordinary.

But the domestic is in itself now a blurred concept. If the territory of the home is defined by the use and display of the designed object as it has been down the years, what are we to make of the adornment of the car, or the way that people are said to feel about their automobiles? What, too, are we to make of the clothes that translate from one area to another. The sports clothes in the city. The army surplus in the clubs? The objects which accompany us from home to work? The phones, faxes, communicators and pagers that make the space in which we work simply everywhere. If the natural antithesis of work has always been home, what are we to make of the phenomenon of home working and the home office? What of the coming revolution in both human behaviour and the design of objects caused by the seemingly unavoidable collision of the computer, the phone and the television?

With that change in the ways in which we are able to communicate underway, the notion of geography and belonging shifts its emphasis. If communications technology begins to make nonsense of geography then where we are ceases to matter as much as it once did. Perversely, at the same time and in a different way, where you are begins to matter an awful lot. In the shifting tides of nets, webs and global telecoms, the real things which make our lives comfortable and bearable take on an even more poignant and perhaps powerful significance. In this shifting world, design matters.

The idea of home, the idea of the domestic is then the location for everything that is significant on the most personal of levels. Arguably, this encompasses ideas such as love, family, language, location, and a sense of a collectively shared past. In the absence of the recognizable national styles which drove Hermann Muthesius to attempt to catalogue the English method of designing for domesticity, we look not for clues to national origin, although those concerns still shape the way that some designers think and work, but instead for the ways in which objects speak to us about their function and their potential role in our lives.

The definition of the domestic is therefore far from being the fixed category it once was and the opportunities for the redefinition of domesticity lie with the theoreticians certainly, but also with the designers and manufacturers represented in these pages. There are many objects in this book, some of which belong to the traditional domestic sphere, some of which do not.

Take for example Bär and Knell's 12 Time Documents; these are chairs that are not chairs, in the sense that they are designed to be made from the reclaimed plastics that we often unthinkingly discard. The intention is for these items of furniture to act as a piece of undisposable agit-prop, a kind of zombie furniture made from the corpse of some other designed object. The point being that this material doesn't just go away when it's thrown away. Many may not like the prospect of having a constant reminder of the wastefulness of our culture in their living rooms, but it is undoubtedly important that this work exists and is seen. This is furniture as a political gesture.

N2's bookshelf is of basic composition and is allied to the shift in living patterns that seems to be occuring in Europe. This is not a piece of furniture that would sit well amongst the fripperies and frills of the standard middle class home. The stripped back aesthetic where materials and composition are the defining characteristics means that this furniture demands the frame of a sparsely furnished modern home. The difference between this piece of furniture and others which have played the same game in the past, is that today these spaces actually exist and are occupied by people who are interested in furniture. Well, sometimes, at least. The same might apply to Michael Young whose development of a formal language which successfully mixes the desire for a kind of hybrid retro with the need for something new has steered furniture design along a new route.

Frogdesign's Power Mac Model illustrates a different approach to the grey box phenomenon which has dominated much of computer design since the MacIntosh's inception in 1984. If the computer is to live in the home, then it has to display characteristics which are not like those of a machine designed for the workplace. Then again, in many instances, workplaces are shifting their character towards the domestic. Equally, Nigel Coates' Legover Chair forms a provocative agenda of its own in terms of form, function and titling. Jasper Morrison's Atlas Table features a tapered leg conceived in a moment of blind invention where sunlight refracted off an existing design and created the same effect.

Gerald Brandstatter's Microwaved Cardboard Scooter takes an object type and forms it using a material not usually connected with transport or toys. It's not clear whether the scooter would stand up to the protracted punishment that would be meted out by the average five year old but the gesture is clear in terms of the hierarchies of materials and the relatively harmless qualities of compacted paper.

Argelik's direct drive motor washing machine with drawer space is from Turkey and is worthy of note if only for the fact that one of the newest additions to the EU is finding a voice in terms of industrial design.

These are all objects which didn't make the main selection. The debates and arguments which surrounded the selection process were often illuminating, enjoyable and infuriating, which is precisely as it should be. The principal point to take away from even the most cursory glance at **The International Design Yearbook 1998** is that this book is by no means complete and it never can. But it at least flags the fact that the way we shape our culture is important and should be seen as such. This book is the snapshot of design for domestic use for 1998, and will be referred to as such by our successors. All that remains to say is that it will be interesting to see what form it takes next year.

Michael Horsham

Furniture

Furniture is the functional dressing of inhabited space.
Which way do we face in homes where heat feels as though it comes from everywhere?
Chairs were once habitually grouped around the fire, now chairs are habitually grouped around the television.
What is wrong with sitting on the floor?
Owning furniture is a sign. But of what?
How do you feel about decorated furniture, or furniture as decoration?
Choosing a bed with your partner, or any other piece of furniture, is a binding contract.
That said, is the sofa a shrine to togetherness?
Storage systems are now domestic furniture.
Furniture defines the home as a space in which to live.

James Irvine
Sofa-bed – Gyro
polyurethane foam – steel frame
h 78cm – l 204cm – d 94cm/75cm
h 30 3/4in – l 80 3/8in – d 37in/29 1/2in
Campeggi – Italy

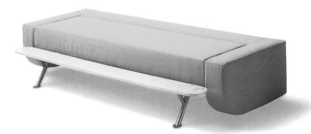

Vico Magistretti
Sofa-bed — Ospite
maple — linen — polyester
h 109cm/66cm — l 210cm/13cm — d 81cm
h 42 7/8in/26in — l 82 5/8in/5 1/8in — d 31 7/8in
Campeggi — Italy

Marzio Rusconi and Swami Anand
Life Meditation Chair and Table – Om and Hari
fibreglass
Chair – h 50cm – l 65cm – d 80cm
    h 19 5/8in – l 25 5/8in – d 31 1/2in
Table – h 46cm – l 128cm – d 117cm
    h 18 1/8in – l 50 3/8in – d 46in
Kundalini – Italy
limited batch production

David Lynch
Table — Club
stained pine — steel
h 61cm — w 24cm — l 24cm
h 24in — w 9 3/8in — l 9 3/8in
Casanostra — Switzerland

Table — Floating Beam
stained pine — steel
h 45cm w 69cm l 90cm
h 17 3/4in — w 27 1/8in — l 35 3/8in
Casanostra — Switzerland

"Coffee in an asymmetrical world"
— David Lynch, USA

Table – Steel Block
stained pine – steel
h 33cm w 40cm l 40cm
h 13in – w 15 3/4in – l 15 3/4in
Casanostra – Switzerland

Table – Espresso
stained pine – steel
h 33cm – w 32cm – l 46cm
h 13in – w 12 5/8in – l 18 1/8in
Casanostra – Switzerland

David Lynch, the famous film director, designs furniture.
Curious, dark little pieces which serve less to deliver
a satisfying experience than unsettle a little with their
perverse but rigorous geometry, their underscale size
and their occasional inherent instability. This is furniture
as a throwback from a never built but often imagined
office complex.

Massimo Morozzi
Storage System – Paesaggi Italiani
rosewood/teak/birch – glass
Edra Mazzei – Italy

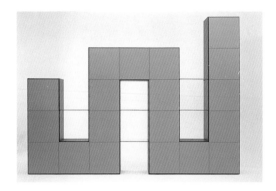 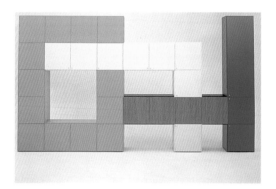

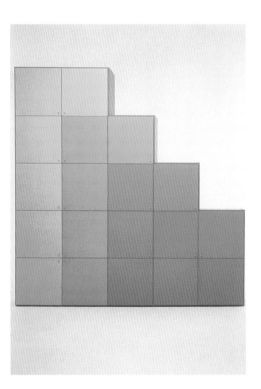

Barbora Skorpilová
Chair – Through and Through
stainless steel – fabric
h 90cm – w 60cm – l 80cm
h 35 3/8in – w 23 5/8in – l 31 1/2in
Messenger Service – Czech Republic
prototype

If there are formal similarities in Starck's and Skorpilová's approach they are accidental. Skorpilová is Czech and works out of Prague, Philippe Starck you know already. The presence of Czech design in these pages is evidence of a small but intensive scene based mostly around the capital. Starck's mutation of a traditional form is intelligent as usual.

Philippe Starck
Rocking Chair – Monsieur X
beech
h 88cm – w 55cm
h 34 5/8in – w 21 5/8in
XO – France

Philippe Starck
Table and Chair – Monsieur X
beech
Table – h 72cm – w 70cm – d 70cm
      h 28 3/8in – w 27 1/2in – d 27 1/2in
Chair – h 88cm – w 55cm – d 48cm
      h 34 5/8in – w 21 5/8in – d 18 7/8in
XO – France

Philippe Starck
Chaise Longue – Monsieur X
beech
h 84cm – w 55cm – l 115cm
h 33in – w 21 5/8in – l 45 3/8in
XO – France

Vico Magistretti
Chaise Longue/Bed – Charlotte
maple – steel – cotton
h 46cm – l 210cm – d 76cm
h 18 1/8in – l 82 5/8in – d 29 7/8in
Campeggi – Italy

Ewa Wolk-Lewanowicz
Chair – Moebius Strip
steel – leather – foam
h 88cm – l 60cm – d 38cm
h 34 5/8in – l 23 5/8in – d 15in
Argento 925 – Poland
limited batch production

Thomas Ferwagner
Chaise – Lazy
stainless steel
h 100cm – w 80cm – l 170cm
h 39 3/8in – w 31 1/2in – l 66 7/8in
Cablevision – Germany

Egon Eiermann
Lounge Chair – E10
rattan
h 80cm – di 80cm
h 31 1/2in – di 31 1/2in
Lampert + Sudrow – Germany

Herbert Hirche
Chair – Santa Lucia
rattan – steel tube
h 72cm – l 49cm – d 53.5cm
h 28 3/8in – l 19 1/4in – d 21in
Lampert + Sudrow – Germany

Poul Kjaerholm
Easy Chair – PKO
laminated wood
h 89cm – w 64cm – d 68cm
h 35in – w 25 1/8in – d 26 3/4in
Fritz Hansen – Denmark

Kjaerholm's two piece black wonder was originally only
a maquette when it was first designed in the fifties. The
technology did not exist then to make it a reality in wood.
This chair is a limited edition anniversary model issued
by Fritz Hansen.

Verner Panton
Chair – Pantoflex Swing
beech – steel
h 84cm – w 52cm – d 54cm
h 33in – w 20 1/2in – d 21 1/4in
VS Vereinigte Spezialmöbelfabriken – Germany

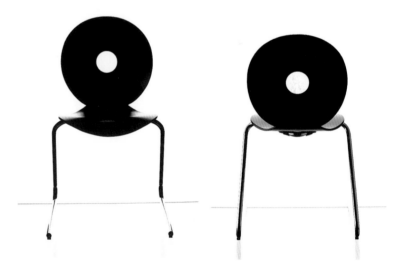

Henrik Frederiksen
Chair
carbon fibre – epoxy – pvc foam
h 80cm – w 62cm – d 60cm
h 31 1/2in – w 24 3/8in – d 23 5/8in
prototype

Niels Hvass
Chair – Flight
aluminium
h 75cm – w 40cm – d 45cm
h 29 1/2in – w 15 3/4in – d 17 3/4in
Källemo – Sweden

Ross Lovegrove
Stacking Chair – Magic
polyurethane – steel
h 80cm – w 55cm – d 56cm
h 31 1/2in – w 21 5/8in – d 22in
Fasem – Italy

Ron Arad
Stacking Chair – FPE Chair
extruded aluminium – thermoplastic technopolymer
h 78cm – w 40cm – d 55cm
h 30 3/4in – w 15 3/4in – d 21 5/8in
Kartell – Italy

Andrew Tye
Chair – Flo
aluminium – bleached oak
h 85cm – w 49cm – d 51cm
h 33 1/2in – w 19 1/4in – d 20in
limited batch production

Philippe Starck
Stacking Chair – Cheap Chic
polypropylene – aluminium
h 80cm – w 44cm – d 52cm
h 31 1/2in – w 17 3/8in – d 20 1/2in
XO – France

Kuno Nüssli and Valerie Kiock – N2
Chair
poplar and birch plywood – mattress springs – ball
h 66cm – w 73cm – d 64cm
h 26in – w 28 3/4in – d 25 1/8in
prototype

This rocking chair is comfortable, though it is made from unyielding wood in a box construction.

Timo Salli
Chair – Tramp
steel – nylon net – zip fastener
h 88cm – w 67cm – d 91cm
h 34 5/8in – w 26 3/8in – d 35 7/8in
Muotoilutoimisto Salli – Finland
limited batch production

"N2 is named after the highway between Lucerne and Basle, although we mostly travel by train for ecological reasons. The group was planned to be our own feedback platform and a vehicle to go public; even for financial matters we needed to come together to face bigger tasks. Our weekly meetings were wild, unstructured, constructive, sometimes the meetings went on until early morning.
We were discovered by Alfred Maurer, manager of the Interni showroom at the furniture fair in Milano. He wanted to promote young Swiss design....without even asking us he booked N2 into Milano......."
– N2, Switzerland

Teppo Asikainen and Ilkka Terho
Rocking Divan – Chip
form pressed birch plywood – pu foam
h 37cm – l 140cm – d 60cm
h 14 5/8in – l 55 1/8in – d 23 5/8in
Oy Netsurfer – Finland

"Chip may stand against the wall in a cramped studio or it can be used to sunbathe or even swing. The consumer becomes a curious child. Uncertainty turns to laughter. Demanding, nihilistic pieces originally created for the designers' needs create surprises and fun in the strangest places."
— Teppo Asikainen and Ilkka Terho, Finland

Henk Vos
Low Chair
aluminium – injected foam – wool
h 78cm – w 67cm – d 100cm
h 30 3/4in – w 26 3/8in – d 39 3/8in
Gelderland Furniture – The Netherlands
limited batch production

Matthew Hilton
Armchair
polyurethane – steel
h 84cm – w 94cm – d 82.5cm
h 33in – w 37in – d 32 1/2in
Driade – Italy

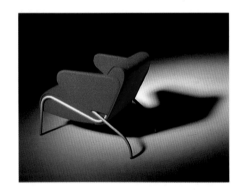

Antonio Citterio and Oliver Loew
Folding Chair – Dolly
fibreglass-filled toughened polypropylene – multi-ply beech
h 94cm/81cm – w 53cm – d 55cm/16cm
h 37in/31 7/8in – w 20 7/8in – d 21 5/8in/6 1/4in
Kartell – Italy

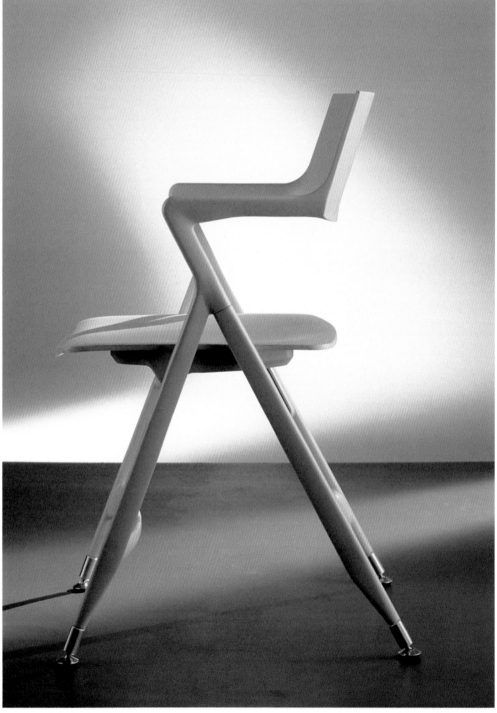

Josep Lluscà
Chair – Scolastica
tubular steel – beech plywood
h 79cm – w 57cm – d 57cm
h 31 1/8in – w 22 3/8in – d 22 3/8in
Fedra – Switzerland

Ilkka Suppanen
Chair – Nomad
steel – felt
h 85cm – w 75cm – d 74cm
h 33 1/2in – w 29 1/2in – d 29 1/8in
prototype

Ilkka Suppanen and Pasi Kolhonen
Chair – Airbag
eps balls – nylon
h 76cm – w 80cm – d 85cm
h 29 7/8in – w 31 1/2in – d 33 1/2in
Snow – Finland

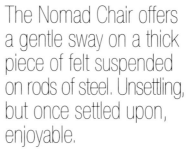

The Nomad Chair offers
a gentle sway on a thick
piece of felt suspended
on rods of steel. Unsettling,
but once settled upon,
enjoyable.

Jeong Myungchul
Table and Chair Set – Tea for Two
lacquered aluminium – chromed steel – birch – beech/cherry
h 72cm – w 60cm – d 60cm
h 28 3/8in – w 23 5/8in – d 23 5/8in
Atlantis – Italy

Rud Thygesen and Johnny Sørensen
Bar Stool – Partout
laminated beech or mahogany
h 99cm/80cm – di 40cm
h 39in/31 1/2in – di 15 3/4in
Magnus Olesen – Denmark

Setsu Ito
Table – Saita
steel
h 75cm – l 100cm – d 70cm
h 29 1/2in – l 39 3/8in – d 27 1/2in
Front Corporation – Japan

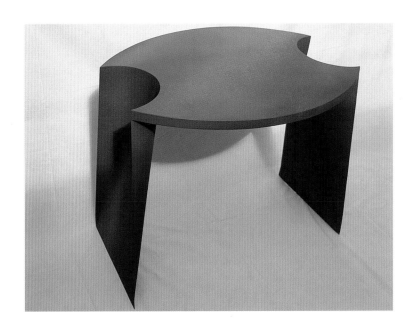

Enzo Mari
Bookcase – Ulm
aluminium – steel
various sizes
Zanotta – Italy

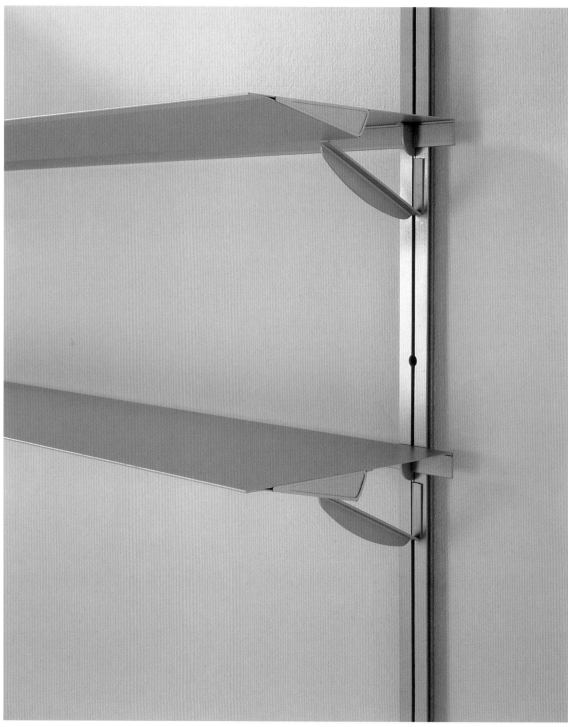

Konstantin Grcic
Shelving – Dinamico
steel
h 154cm – w 38cm – d 29cm
h 60 5/8in – w 15in – d 11 3/8in
Fedra – Switzerland

Konstantin Grcic
Shelving – Zig Zag
tubular and bent steel
h 202cm/88cm – w 150cm – d 33cm
h 79 1/2in/34 5/8in – w 59in – d 13in
Fedra – Switzerland

Kurt Greter
Cupboard – Treibhaus
plexiglas – anodized aluminium
h 200cm – w 60cm – d 60cm
h 78 3/4in – w 23 5/8in – d 23 5/8in
Atelier Greter – Switzerland

Pastoe/Wogg
Cupboard – Match
birch veneer – polystyrene
h 200cm – w 37cm – d 37cm
h 78 3/4in – w 14 5/8in – d 14 5/8in
UMS-Pastoe – The Netherlands

Franz-Josef Schulte
Bookcase – LeseLust
fibreboard
h 196cm – w 100cm – d 45cm
h 77 1/8in – w 39 3/8in – d 17 3/4in
Schulte Design – Germany

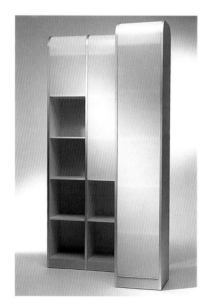

Daniele Lo Scalzo Moscheri
Bookcase – Crossline
aluminium – laminate – cherrywood
h (max) 209cm – w 95cm/65cm – d 39cm
h (max) 82 1/4in – w 37 3/8in/25 5/8in – d 15 3/8in
Elam – Italy

Christopher Procter and Fernando Rihl
Storage System – Topo
birch plywood – plastic
h 200cm – w 200cm – d 30cm
h 78 3/4in – w 78 3/4in – d 11 3/4in
Spatial Interference – UK
limited batch production

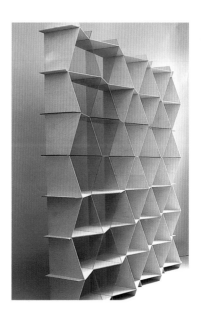

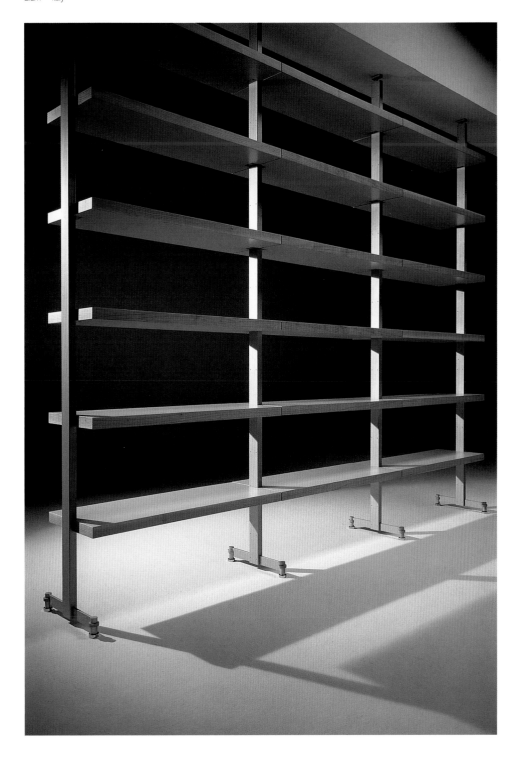

Jakob Berg
Stacking Chair – Flow
birch plywood
h 83cm – w 40cm – d 50cm
h 32 5/8in – w 15 3/4in – d 19 5/8in
prototype

Rud Thygesen
Stool
ash
h 42cm – w 44cm – d 27cm
h 16 1/2in – w 17 3/8in – d 10 5/8in
Roth Andersen – Denmark

Rud Thygesen
Armchair
ash
h 70cm – w 56cm – d 38cm
h 27 1/2in – w 22in – d 15in
Danish Technological Institute
prototype

Roderick Vos (Studio Maupertuus)
Side Table – Squares
mdf – laminated birch
h 40cm – w 40cm – d 40cm
h 15 3/4in – w 15 3/4in – d 15 3/4in
Horas International – Belgium
limited batch production

Tom Bisig and Nicole Naas
Shelves
birch plywood – galvanized wire
h 208cm – w 95cm – d 33.5cm
h 81 7/8in – w 37 3/8in – d 13 1/8in
Atelier Alinea – Switzerland

William Sawaya
Bookshelves – Ex Libris
wood – metal
h 210cm – l 152cm – d 40cm
h 82 5/8in – l 59 7/8in – d 15 3/4in
Sawaya + Moroni – Italy

Ilkka Suppanen
Cupboard – AV
steel – glass – woven steel – plastic
h 150cm – w 70cm – d 50cm
h 59in – w 27 1/2in – d 19 5/8in
Snow – Finland
limited batch production

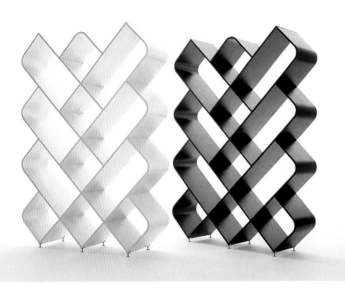

Shin and Tomoko Azumi
Bench/Bed
beech — sprayed mdf
h 54cm/27cm – l 190cm – d 48cm/80cm
h 21 1/4in/10 5/8in – l 74 3/4in – d 18 7/8in/31 1/2in
one-off

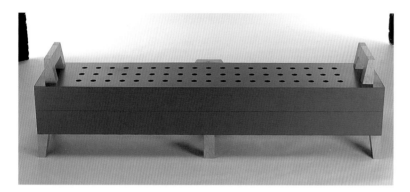

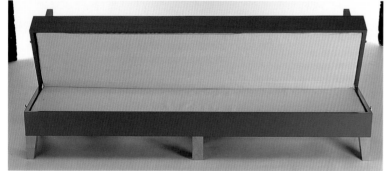

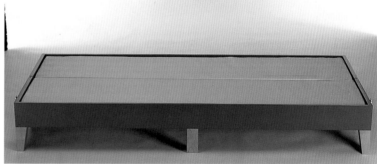

Perhaps inspired by the need for space in the modern home all over the globe, the bench that converts into the bed is not a new idea, but here it is well executed in an understated way.

Roberto Lucci and Paolo Orlandini
Sofa-bed – Park
upholstery – steel – wood
h 80cm – w 160cm – d 85cm
h 31 1/2in – w 63in – d 33 1/2in
Biesse – Italy

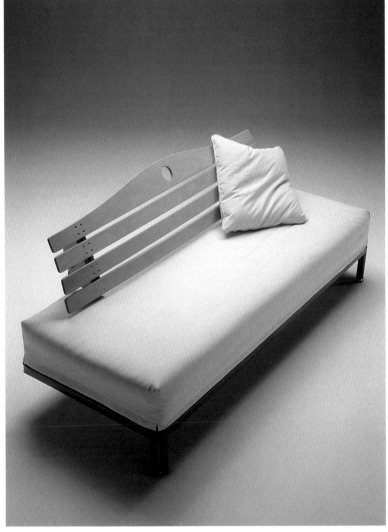

Norbert Wangen
Kitchen
wood – stone – steel
h 93cm – w 62cm – d 106–220cm
h 36 5/8in – w 24 3/8in – d 41 3/4–86 5/8in
prototype

Minimal, space-saving kitchen.

Jos Laugs
Table – Robin
maple veneer – mdf – aluminium
h 74cm – w 95cm – l 190cm
h 29 1/8in – w 37 3/8in – l 74 3/4in
Montis – The Netherlands

Katie Walker
Console Table
cherrywood
h 85cm – w 50cm – l 150cm
h 33 1/2in – w 19 5/8in – l 59in
limited batch production

Katie Walker
Gallery Seating
ash – steel – leather
h 45.5cm – w 55cm – l 200cm
h 17 7/8in – w 21 5/8in – l 78 3/4in
limited batch production

David Braun – N2
Bed – HDB
wood – futon
h 10–14cm – l 190cm – d 150cm
h 3 7/8–5 1/2in – l 74 3/4in – d 59in
prototype

This Reber – N2
Screen
wood – aluminium
h 180cm – w 40–160cm – d 4–12cm
h 70 7/8in – w 15 3/4–63in – d 1 5/8–4 3/4in
prototype

Konstantin Grcic
Chest of Drawers – Mania
maple veneer – macroter
h 113cm/93cm – w 72cm/36cm – d 48cm
h 44 1/2in/36 5/8in – w 28 3/8in/14 1/8in – d 18 7/8in
ClassiCon – Germany

Jörg Boner – N2
Cupboard
mdf – polished aluminium
h 180cm – w 60cm – d 60cm
h 70 7/8in – w 23 5/8in – d 23 5/8in
prototype

Gio Ponti
Bookcase – Elena
cherrywood
h 100cm – w 90cm – d 21cm
h 39 3/8in – w 35 3/8in – d 8 1/4in
Costantino – Italy

Caroline Casey
Folding screen
rock maple veneer plywood – solid wood
h 200cm – l 150cm – d 3cm
h 78 3/4in – l 59in – d 1 1/8in
limited batch production

Norbert Wangen
Chair/Table
cherrywood – steel
chair – h 75cm – w 50cm – d 64cm
    h 29 1/2in – w 19 5/8in – d 25 1/8in
table – h 41cm – w 100cm/50cm – d 93cm
    h 16 1/8in – w 39 3/8in/19 5/8in – d 36 5/8in
Norbert Wangen – Germany

Norbert Wangen
Sofa-bed
cherrywood – steel
Bench – h 75cm – l 200cm – d 64cm
    h 29 1/2in – l 78 3/4in – d 25 1/8in
Bed – h 41cm – l 200cm – d 93cm
    h – 16 1/8in – l 78 3/4in – d 36 5/8in
Norbert Wangen – Germany

Julia Rosengarth
Bench – Bank 2
maple – steel – zinc
h 77cm – l 158cm – d 60cm
h 30 3/8in – l 62 1/4in – d 23 5/8in
Fritz Möbel – Germany

David Field
Meeting Table
pearwood
h 72cm – w 110cm – l 110cm
h 28 3/8in – w 43 1/4in – l 43 1/4in
Opus Magnum – UK
one-off

Helmut Galler
Bedstead – Nr 1700
beech – birch multiplex
h 28cm – l 203cm – d 90cm
h 11in – l 79 7/8in – d 35 3/8in
Schmidinger Modul Wohn + Objektbedarf – Austria

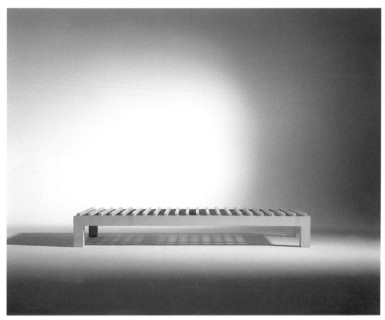 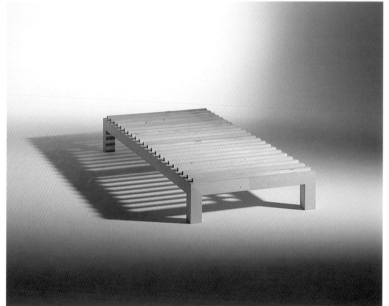

A minimal bed.

Noa Hanyu
Table – Shutaku 29
wood
h 19cm – w 114cm – d 79cm
h 7 1/2in – w 44 7/8in – d 31 1/8in
one-off

Shinichi Sumikawa
Chest – Dandan
japanese lacquered wood
h 36cm – w 36cm – d 12cm
h 14 1/8in – w 14 1/8in – d 4 3/4in
Amano Shikki Co. – Japan

Ruud-Jan Kokke
Stool – TC
plywood
h 45cm – w 36cm
h 17 3/4in – w 14 1/8in
Designum – The Netherlands

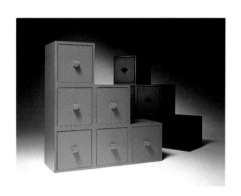

Rud Thygesen and Johnny Sørensen
Sofa – Duo
bent laminated beech
h 80cm – l 122cm – d 65cm
h 31 1/4in – l 48in – d 25 5/8in
Magnus Olesen – Denmark

Olgoj Chorchoj – Michal Fronek and Jan Nemecek
Bench for Ústí nad Labem
cast metal – wood
h 85cm – l 180cm – d 59cm
h 33 1/2in – l 70 7/8in – d 23 1/4in
Langer – Czech Republic

Manolo Portaceli
Low Table – Charo
cherrywood
h 43cm – di 110cm
h 16 7/8in – di 43 1/4in
Punt Mobles – Spain

Olgoj Chorchoj – Michal Fronek and Jan Nemecek
Table – Round Oblong
wood – glass
h 40cm – l 100cm – d 60cm
h 15 3/4in – l 39 3/8in – d 23 5/8in
one-off

A thick, cold cast glass table top transforms this
table into an item with a surprising mass. A desirable,
handworked object.

Jakob Gebert
Table – Spanoto
birch plywood – linoleum – wood veneer
h 74cm – l 220cm/190cm/160cm – d 86cm
h 29 1/8in – l 86 5/8in/74 3/4in/63in – d 33 7/8in
Moormann Möbel und Handels – Germany

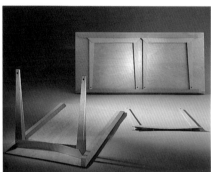

Svitalia Design
Wall cabinet – Jenseits
plywood beech – aluminium
h 40cm – l 120cm – d 18cm
h 15 3/4in – l 47 1/4in – d 7 1/8in
prototype

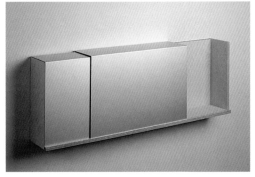

Michele de Lucchi
Cupboard System – Sistemare
steel – wood – glass – textile
h 78–191cm – w 80–120cm – d 43cm
h 30 3/4–75 1/4in – w 31 1/2–47 1/4in – d 16 7/8in
Mauser – Germany

"I mainly work for industries. I cannot judge my work but I always try to bridge human need and companies' conveniences, ecological consciousness and business, philosophy and market research, progress and investment limitations, art and functionality, beauty and comfort, freedom of choice and production limitations, experimentation and concreteness, sensuality and technology, optimism and economic crisis, education and consumerism, happiness and a stressful life, contemplation and speed, intimacy and status, domesticity and public relations......."
– Michele de Lucchi, Italy

Lighting

Electric lighting is the sign of civilization.
A swathe of electric light is visible from space which sweeps from the north of England down through the centre of Europe to Spain.
Light is a psychoactive material.
Light is wave and particle.
Light is time.
The presentation and delivery of light in the home is an essentially modern arena of design.
Luminescence is seductive.
Unlike other categories, all of the objects in this section perform exactly the same function.
Differentiation is in material and form.

Masayo Ave
Table Lamp — Moran
metal — polyester
9w energy-saving bulb
h 30cm — di 30cm
h 11 3/4in — di 11 3/4in
Ave Design Corporation — Italy
limited batch production

Sergio Asti
Suspension Light – Inao
murano glass – metal
max. 150w halogen E27 bulb
h 36cm – di 50cm
h 14 1/8in – di 19 5/8in
I Tre – Italy

Juan Gaspar
Suspension Light – Gran Via
glass – metal
2 x 100w E27 bulbs
h 40cm – di 42cm
h 15 3/4in – di 16 1/2in
Marset Iluminacion – Spain

Frans van Nieuwenborg
Table Lamp and Wall Light – The Saint
aluminium – plastic
22w circular fluorescent tube
h 30cm – w 25cm – l 25cm
h 11 7/8in – w 9 7/8in – l 9 7/8in
Van Nieuwenborg Industrial Design Consultancy Group – The Netherlands

Achille Castiglioni
Suspension Light – Fucsia
blown glass – translucent silicone 40w E14 R50 bulbs with 1 – 3 – 8 or 12 diffusers
diffuser – h 35cm – di 16cm
          h 13 3/4in – di 6 1/4in
Flos – Italy

Matteo Thun
Suspension Light – La Trave
aluminium – plastic – steel
T26 (T8) or T16 (T5) fluorescent bulb
h 16cm – w 33cm – l 170cm
h 6 1/4in – w 13in – l 66 7/8in
Zumtobel Licht – Austria

Shin Azumi
Table Lamp – Dimming with Movement
beechwood – fire-retardant paper
40w bulb
h 40cm – di 22cm
h 15 3/4in – di 8 5/8in
Azumi's Planning Co – UK
limited batch production

Sigeaki Asahara
Recessed Spots – Kridue
die-cast aluminium – glass
max. 50w 12v dichroic bulb
w 9cm – l 8cm – d 7cm
w 3 1/2in – l 3 1/8in – d 2 3/4in
Lucitalia – Italy

Tobias Grau and Peter Sonntag
Spotlight – OMM
high-tech synthetics
35–50w bulb
di 13.5cm
di 5 3/8in
Tobias Grau – Germany

Ingo Maurer and Team
Suspension Light – MozzNik
12 x 50w halogen bulbs
h 100cm – di 180–220cm
h 39 3/8in – di 70 7/8–86 5/8in
Ingo Maurer – Germany

Grazia Azzolin
Wall Light – Chiara
metal – thermoformed glass
max. 200w halogen bulb
h 52.5cm – w 37cm – d 13.5cm
h 20 5/8in – w 14 1/2in – d 5 3/8in
Renato Fabbian & Co. – Italy

Stephen Philips
Desk Light – Cape Light
polypropylene – steel press-studs
40w 230–240v bulb
h 44cm – w 21cm – l 29cm
h 17 3/8in – w 8 1/4in – l 11 3/8in
Stephen Philips Design – UK

"The Cape Light is a response to an ever increasing number of people who, due to urban congestion and for economic reasons, choose to work at home. I have tried to resolve the formal, visual and technical problems associated with these dual activities. The light either directly illuminates tasks, or by rotating the head it diffuses light off the wall for a more relaxed domestic environment."
– Stephen Philips, UK

Lighting

Tatsuro Funahashi
Table Lamp – Leaf Light
acrylic plate – oak
30w krypton bulb
h 28cm – w 25cm – d 15cm
h 11in – w 9 7/8in – d 5 7/8in
Chubu Design Research Center Co. – Japan

Jasper Startup
Ceiling Light – Miss
plywood
16w compact fluorescent
h 33cm – di 25cm
h 13in – di 9 7/8in
Startup Design – UK
limited batch production

John and Penny Smith
Wall Light – Olympus Series
porcelain – timber veneer – metal
low-energy miniature fluorescent bulbs
h 100cm – w 30cm – d 15cm
h 39 3/8in – w 11 7/8in – d 5 7/8in
prototype

Ayala Sperling-Serfaty
Suspension Light – Eight Palms
silk – organza – metal
8 x 75w E27 bulbs
h 100cm – di 130cm
h 39 3/8in – di 51 1/8in
Aqua Creations – Israel
one-off

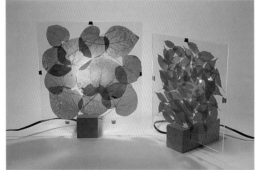

Sigeaki Asahara
Wall Light – Stresa G Flat
glass – technopolymers
150w incandescent or halogen E27 or
23w electronic fluorescent E27
h 26cm – w 38cm – d 20cm
h 10 1/4in – w 15in – d 7 7/8in
Lucitalia – Italy

Julian Powell-Tuck
Floodlight – Event
aluminium
18–26w compact fluorescent or 150w halogen bulb
various sizes
Concord Lighting – UK

Sigeaki Asahara
Lighting System – Modulex 150
die-cast aluminium
various light sources
h 12–23cm – di 16cm
h 4 3/4–9in – di 6 1/4in
Ushio Spax – Japan

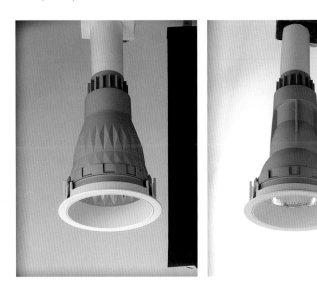

Manel Ybargüengoitia
Table Lamps 1 + 2 – Eliana
brass – zamack
13w fluorescent bulb
table lamp 1 – h 52cm/23cm – w 82cm/62cm
        h 20 1/2in/9in – w 32 3/8in/24 3/8in
table lamp 2 – h 84cm – w 20cm
        h 33 1/8in – w 7 7/8in
B. Lux – Spain

Josep Lluscà
Lighting System – Tekno G
stainless steel – crystal – polycarbonate
left – 10–20w 12v G4 halogen bulb
        h 9cm – w 12cm
        h 3 1/2in – w 4 3/4in
right –11w G23 halogen bulb
        h 9cm – w 33.5cm
        h 3 1/2in – w 13 1/8in
Blauet – Spain

M+T Team
Floor Lamp – Cai
metal – leather – parchment-like material
max. 150w E27 bulb
h 136–180cm – di 50cm
h 53 1/2–70 7/8in – di 19 5/8in
Marset Iluminación – Spain

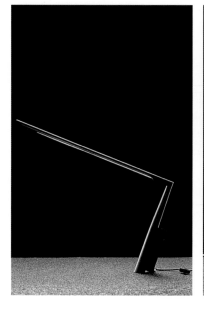

Antoine Cahen
Torch — XL Light
plastic
l 10cm — di 2cm
h 3 7/8in — di 3/4in
Leclanche — Switzerland

Andrea Anselmi and Corrado Baglioni
Table Lamp — Santamaria from set Le Tre Caravelle
metal — wood
100w 230v E27 bulb
h 58cm — di 30cm
h 22 7/8in — di 11 3/4in
Iduna — Italy

Erwin Egli
Floor Lamp – Trapez
steel – pressure-cast aluminium
36w/58w bulb
h 166.5cm/136.5cm
h 65 1/2in/53 3/4in
Ribag Licht – Switzerland

Herbert H. Schultes
Floor Lamp – Nisos
metal – glass
max. 60w E14 bulb
h 175cm – di 27cm
h 68 7/8in – di 10 5/8in
ClassiCon – Germany

Adrien Gardere
Floor Lamp – Corner Lamp
textured metacrylic – beechwood – tubular steel
15w low-temperature fluorescent bulb
h 170cm – w 22cm – d 22cm
h 66 7/8in – w 8 5/8in – d 8 5/8in
Roset – France

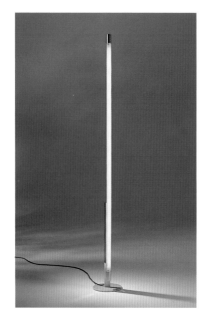

Erwin Egli
Suspension Light – Trapez
steel – abs
18 – 36 or 58w bulb
l 159.5cm/129.5cm/68.5cm
l 62 3/4in/51in/27in
Ribag Licht – Switzerland

Anne Kosonen and Helena Mattila-Sorri
Table Lamp – Friends' Village
metal or wood – carton
40w 220v bulb
h 40–50cm – w 18cm – d 18cm
h 15 3/4–19 5/8in – w 7in – d 7in
Everyday Design – Finland
limited batch production

Thomas Zawalski
Garden Light – Vento
high-grade steel – plastic – polypropylene
candle
h 163cm – di 11cm
h 64 1/8in – di 4 3/8in
Zaket – Germany

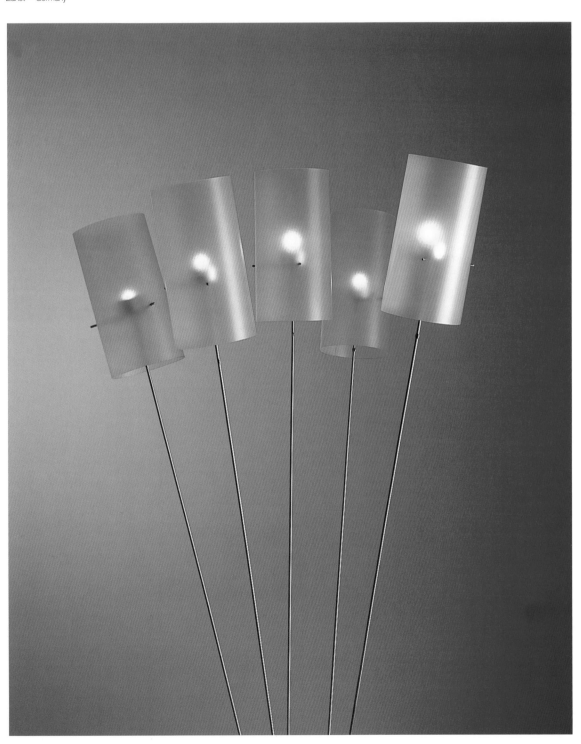

Winfried Scheuer
Suspension Light – LiteLite
polypropylene
60w bulb
h 20cm – di 35cm
h 7 7/8in – di 13 3/4in
Zaket – Germany

Michele de Lucchi
Table Lamp – Treforchette
pvc
max. 60w E14 bulb
h 47cm – di 20cm
h 18 1/2in – di 7 7/8in
Produzione Privata – Italy

Jorge Garcia Garay
Wall Light – Casino
iron – metacrylic
18–36w fluorescent G13 bulb
h 8cm – w 10cm – l 130cm/70cm/28cm
h 3 1/8in – w 3 7/8in – l 51 1/8in/27 1/2in/11in
Garcia Garay – Spain

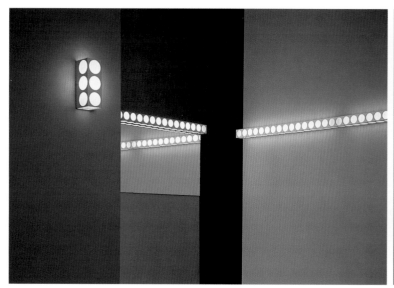

Christian Deuber – N2
Multi-purpose Light
58w fluorescent bulb
synthetic tube – rubber – steel
h 175cm – di 6cm
h 68 7/8in – di 2 3/8in
N2 – Switzerland
prototype

Henrik Lund-Larsen
Floor Lamp – Hood
aluminium – iron
40w Mignon bulb
h 133cm – w 40cm – l 31cm
h 52 3/8in – w 15 3/4in – l 12 1/4in
Unique Interieur – Denmark

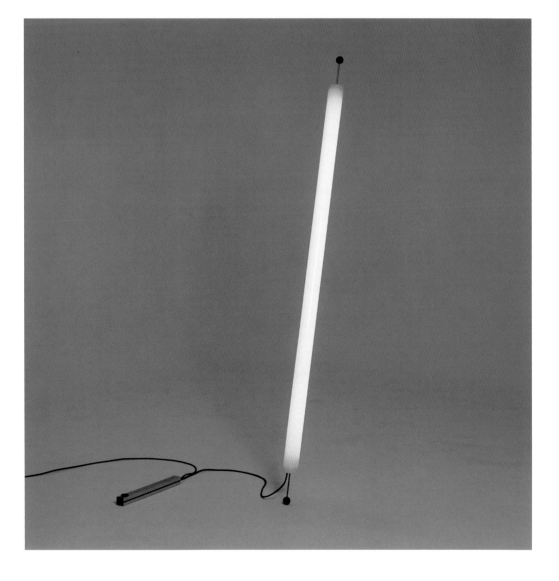

Mario Barbaglia and Marco Colombo
Floor Lamp – Alalunga
painted metal
300w halogen bulb
h 189cm – w 45cm – d 24cm
h 74 3/8in – w 17 3/4in – d 9 3/8in
Italiana Luce – Italy

David D'Imperio
Halogen Light – Duet Table Light
metal – plastic
2 x 20w 12v halogen MR-11 bulbs
h 51cm – w 25cm – d 14cm
h 20in – w 10in – d 5 1/2in
David D'Imperio – USA
limited batch production

Bernard Vuarnesson
Table Lamp – Clips
stainless steel – polypropylene
40w 250v bulb
h 24cm – di 16cm
h 9 3/8in – di 6 1/4in
Sculptures-Jeux – France

Dagmar Mombach – Ingo Maurer and Team
Group of Lights – MoMaNoughies
paper – glass – silicone – plastic – metal
200w 12v halogen bulb
h 105cm – w 50cm – d 50cm
h 41 3/8in – w 19 5/8in – d 19 5/8in
Ingo Maurer – Germany
limited batch production

Dagmar Mombach – Ingo Maurer and Team
Suspension Light – MoMaNoughies
paper – silicone – plastic – metal
50w 12v halogen bulb
h 75cm – w 28cm – d 28cm
h 29 1/2in – w 11in – d 11in
Ingo Maurer – Germany
limited batch production

Tableware

'Tableware' implies a grand tradition of the table as centrepiece.
The table is no longer the locus of the domestic set piece.
Dinner is no longer served at eight.
Tableware is both an anachronism and a necessity.
The vessel is the last bastion of theory in craft.
Vessels are also mass produced in polypropylene.
Ownership of a plate and a knife no longer signifies as high a status in society as it did in the Middle Ages.
Ownership of a plate and knife is nothing without the ownership of a fork and spoon and table.

Olgoj Chorchoj – Michal Fronek and Jan Nemecek
Bowl – Sony
glass
h 7cm – w 21cm – l 40cm
h 2 3/4in – w 8 1/4in – l 15 3/4in
P. & L. Pelechov – Czech Republic
limited batch production

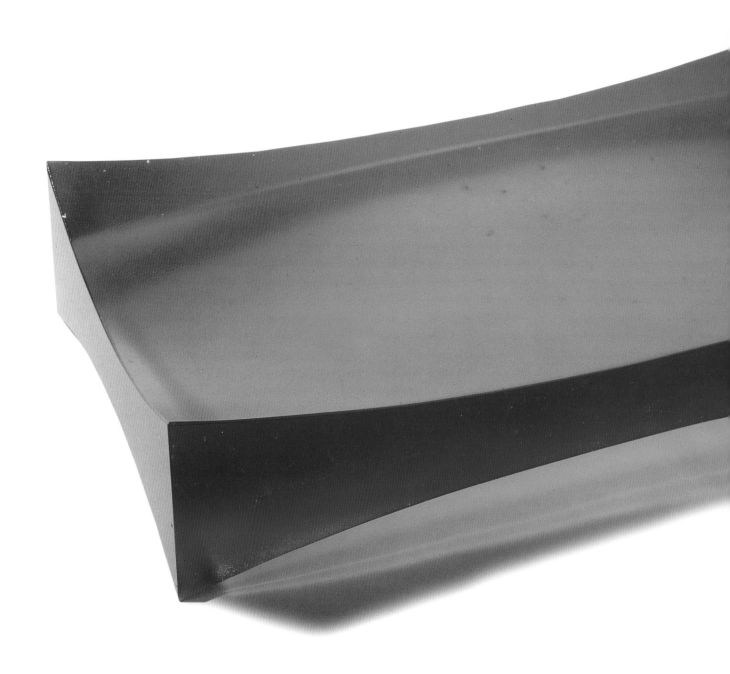

Olgoj Chorchoj's project concerns the re-establishment of Czech traditions in manufacture and form. This bowl is made from cold cast glass, a technique which has all but disappeared from Czech manufacturing. The glass is then hand polished in a laborious process or left with the natural frosting which the technique imparts.

Jos Devriendt
Vase – in three parts
red clay – transparent glaze
h 51cm – di 16cm
h 20in – di 6 1/4in
limited batch production

  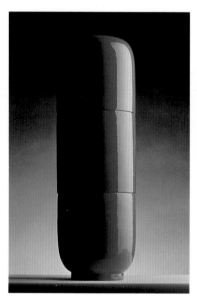 

Carina Andersson
Set of cylinders
glass
h 22.5cm/12.5cm – di 22.5cm/13cm
h 8 7/8in/4 7/8in – di 8 7/8in/5 1/8in
cbi – Sweden

Gill Gane
Bowl
earthenware – clear gloss glaze
h 8.5cm – di 20cm
h 3 3/8in – di 7 7/8in
Neudorf Ceramics – New Zealand
limited batch production

Julie Blyfield
Bowl
anodized aluminium – brass – gold plate
h 8cm – di 11cm
h 3 1/8in – di 4 3/8in
limited batch production (5)

Noa Hanyu
Tray – Moriki
wood
h 6cm – w 92cm – d 52cm
h 2 3/8in – w 36 1/4in – d 20 1/2in
one-off

Tableware

Alfredo Häberli and Christophe Marchand
Centrepiece – Malvinas
steel
Alias – Italy

Olgoj Chorchoj – Michal Fronek and Jan Nemecek
Vase – Jupiter
glass
h 21cm – di 20cm
h 8 1/4in – di 7 7/8in
P + L Pelechov – Czech Republic
limited batch production

"Our approach to design is to fuse together forms and technologies which are related to where we are from and where we are working. That is: the Czech Republic. We are not only interested in the formal languages of the past, but also in the ways that manufacturing here can develop contemporary forms using a combination of the old and the new in terms of materials and technologies. We are equally at home with wood, cold cast glass or lightweight aircraft alloys."
– Michal Fronek, Jan Nemecek – Olgoj Chorchoj, The Czech Republic

Erika Lagerbielke
Vase – Happy Days
crystal
h 13cm
h 5 1/8in
Orrefors–Kosta Boda – Sweden
limited batch production

Annaleena Hakatie
Candleholder – Ballo
pressed glass
h 4.5cm – w 9cm
h 1 3/4in – w 3 1/2in
Iittala – Hackman Designor – Finland

Yellow Design
Coffee Pot, Cup and Plate – from the Vario Series
porcelain
Rosenthal – Germany
various sizes

Masatoshi Sakaegi
Cups, Bowl and Tray – Blue Line
porcelain
cup – h 8cm – w 8cm
       h 3 1/8in – w 3 1/8in
bowl – h 8cm – w 17cm
       h 3 1/8in – w 6 5/8in
tray – h 2cm – w 22.5cm
       h 3/4in – w 8 7/8in
Sakaegi Design Studio – Japan

Erik-Jan Kwakkel
Mugs – Isola
porcelain
h 10.5cm – di 9cm
h 4 1/8in – di 3 1/2in
Goods – The Netherlands

Achille Castiglioni
Table Set – Bravura
porcelain
di 5.5–28cm
di 2 1/8–11in
Alessi – Italy

Enzo Mari
Vase – Camicia
glass – anodized aluminium
h 8cm – di 12cm
h 3 1/8in – di 4 3/4in
Alessi – Italy

Vase/Carafe – Trinidad
handblown glass
h 17cm – di 11.5cm
h 6 5/8in – di 4 1/2in
Alessi – Italy

Enzo Mari
Two Egg Cup/Candleholder Set – Hawaii
melamine
h 6.5cm – di 5.5cm
h 2 1/2in – di 2 1/8in
Alessi – Italy

Parmesan Cheese Container – Java
melamine
h 7cm – di 14.5cm
h 2 3/4in – di 5 3/4in
Alessi – Italy

Salt and Pepper Set – Faraglioni
melamine
h 9cm – di 5.5cm
h 3 1/2in – di 2 1/8in
Alessi – Italy

Enzo Mari
Rectangular Tray – Arran
stainless steel
h 4cm – w 24.5cm – l 48cm
h 1 5/8in – w 9 5/8in – l 18 7/8in
Alessi – Italy

Fruit Bowl – Adal
heat-moulded ps
h 9cm – di 29.5cm
h 3 1/2in – di 11 5/8in
Alessi – Italy

Achille Castiglioni
Fruit Holder – Ondula
stainless steel
h 6cm – di 31.5cm
h 2 3/8in – di 12 3/8in
Alessi – Italy

Enzo Mari
Bread Basket
thermoplastic resin
h 6.5cm – di 21.5cm
h 2 1/2in – di 8 1/2in
Alessi – Italy

Marcel Wanders
Vases
porcelain
h 14–26cm – di 10–18cm
h 5 1/4in–10 1/4in – di 3 7/8–7in
Rosenthal – Germany

Kazuhiko Tomita
Vase – Yao
glass
h 30cm – di 12cm
h 11 3/4in – di 4 3/4in
Arcade – Italy

Barbora Skorpilová
Vase – Zig Zag
glass – stainless steel
h 14cm – w 14cm – d 56cm
h 5 1/2in – w 5 1/2in – d 22in
Interier Maly – Czech Republic

Norberto Medardi and Angelo Gueli
Candlestick – Oirab
brass – harmonic steel wires
h 50cm – di 10cm
h 19 5/8in – di 3 7/8in
Michele Veccia Edizioni Design – Italy

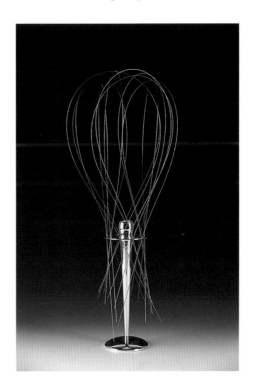

Lars Hellsten
Vase – Butterfly
crystal
h 26cm – di 32cm/28cm
h 10 1/4in – di 12 5/8in/11in
Orrefors–Kosta Boda – Sweden

Lino Sabattini
Vase – Busto
silver
h 27.5cm – l 33cm
h 10 7/8in – l 13in
Sabattini Argenteria – Italy

Barbora Skorpilová
Vase – Reek
glass – Duralumin
h 50cm – di 24cm
h 19 5/8in – di 9 3/8in
Interier Maly – Czech Republic

Janja Lap
Wine Glass – Memory
crystal
h 20.5cm – di 9cm
h 8in – di 3 1/2in
Steklarska Sola – Slovenia
limited batch production

Sergio Asti
Tray for Appetizers or Sweets – Margherita
silver
w 26cm – l 23cm
w 10 1/4in – l 9in
Gabriele de Vecchi – Italy
limited batch production

"All of us have at our disposal an alphabet, and later, once adult, a wholly
personal vocabulary which changes continually. While the alphabet is a freely
provided objective and mechanical instrument, our vocabulary reflects our world,
our anxieties and our labours. The space for the imagination, or for the imaginary,
the space for all that is not a codified and immutable stereotype, is large or
infinite as the case may be. It is a space which is an integral part of our vocabulary.
In fact this space lays down the guidelines for it. Our vocabulary, which
is also our way of being, is therefore difficult to reduce to a unidirectional
interpretation or to a geometric univocality, but instead must be deciphered
and understood as one would a code."
– Sergio Asti, Italy

Marc Harrison
Salt and Pepper Capsules – ANTonyms
stainless steel – rubber
h 2cm – w 3.4cm – l 7cm
h 3/4in – w 1 3/8in – l 2 3/4in
Antworks – Australia

Nick Crosbie
Glass Jar
pvc – glass
h 18cm – di 11cm
h 7in – di 4 3/8in
Inflate – UK

"I have always tried to direct the products towards ordinary people rather than the design conscious, with a focus on everyday chores having more sparkle. Just styling an object is not itself the solution, it is just the final piece of the puzzle. My approach is to do with the repositioning of familiar processes into different contexts. So far this has concerned HF welding in the form of inflatables. By determining the territory anew, the products stand out by themselves."
– Nick Crosbie, Inflate, UK

Nick Crosbie
Sugar Shaker
pvc – stainless steel
h 12cm – di 8cm
h 4 3/4in – di 3 1/8in
Inflate – UK

Geoff Hollington
Candleholders – Palette
glass – rubber
h 17cm/14cm/11cm – di 5.5cm
h 6 5/8in/5 1/2in/4 3/8in – di 2 1/8in
Design Ideas – USA

Thomas Eisl
Sugar Jar
glass – aluminium – stainless steel
h 14cm – w 13cm – d 12cm
h 5 1/2in – w 5 1/8in – d 4 3/4in
one-off

Chanan de-Lange
Vase
aluminium
h 35cm – di 17cm
h 13 3/4in – di 6 5/8in
limited batch production

Norberto Medardi
Candlestick – Oirot
aluminium casting
h 25cm – w 11cm – d 27cm
h 9 7/8in – w 43/8in – d 10 5/8in
Michele Veccia Edizioni Design – Italy

Tatsuro Funahashi
Wire Tray
steel wire
h 5.5cm – w 31cm – d 31cm
h 2 1/8in – w 12 1/4in – d 12 1/4in
Chubu Design Research Center Co. – Japan
limited batch production

Michele de Lucchi
Centrepiece – I Petali
ceramic – metal
h 19cm – di 36cm
h 7 1/2in – di 14 1/8in
Produzione Privata – Italy

Jirí Pelcl
Coffee Cup – Novito
porcelain
h 7.5cm – di 7cm
h 3in – di 2 3/4in
Novito – Czech Republic
limited batch production

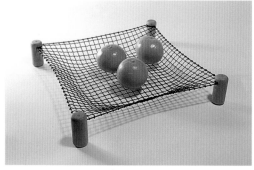

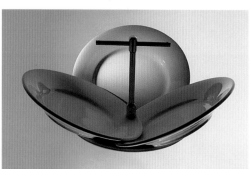

Olgoj Chorchoj – Michal Fronek and Jan Nemecek
Ashtray
duralumin
h 8cm – di 12cm
h 3 1/8in – di 4 3/4in
Artel – Czech Republic

Enzo Mari
Double-Sided Vase – Pago-Pago
abs
h 30.5cm – di 20cm
h 12in – di 7 7/8in
Alessi – Italy

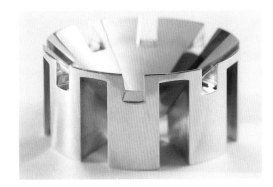

Enzo Mari
Cutlery – Piuma
stainless steel
w 2.5–4cm – l 13.5–22.5cm
w 1–1 5/8in – l 5 3/8–8 7/8in
Zani + Zani – Italy

Strength imparted by the simple expedient of stamping the steel with a profile which ought to prevent spoon-bending. This is a staple treatment in the manufacture of cheap cutlery made of thin alloys. The aesthetic of the factory dining hall crosses over into the home.

Achille and Pier Giacomo Castiglioni
Cutlery Set – Grand Prix
stainless steel
l 10–27.5cm
l 4–10 3/4in
Alessi – Italy

Metz.Schlett.Kindler
Salad Server – Bakaroo
metal
h 2.5cm – w 7cm – l 28cm
h 1in – w 2 3/4in – l 11in
Raffelberg Kollektion – Germany

"To explore orientation to customs, habits and be-havioural patterns learned in time. To look beyond one's own horizon to the necessary and the un-important for new materials and those that are proven. The basis for every product development is to convert these ideas to today's productions – the small scale and the mass produced – without losing sight of logic and simplicity."
– Metz/Schlett/Kindler, Designers, Germany

Jirí Pelcl
Coffee Spoon – Sperm Agnes
porcelain or silver
l 13cm
l 5 1/8in
Novito – Czech Republic

Achille and Pier Giacomo Castiglioni
Spoon for Mayonnaise – Sleek
pmma
l 20cm
l 7 7/8in
Alessi – Italy

Somehow it feels as though we are being offered clues to the state of our civilization when half the world is going hungry and yet we have spoons for specific jobs such as serving salad, spreading mayonnaise and stirring our coffee.

Textiles

Textiles and textile manufacture were at the heart of the industrial revolution.
Textiles are the natural resting place for the illustrative impulse in design.
The use of textiles in the home is conditioned by geographic location.
Decorative textiles demand in the user an empathy with the representation of the drawn mark.
Woven textiles reveal the history of their manufacture in their texture and their composition.
Textile designers are finding work in the field of new media.
Woven textile design demands forethought in structure and layering.
Unlike other media, textiles have the capacity to be an effective three-dimensional print medium.
Textiles offer the possibility to live with illustration.

Kristina Råström
Carpet – Krickan
wool
w 150cm – l 200cm
w 59in – l 78 3/4in
Asplund – Sweden

The rug is the final carrier of the drawn mark. The transference of the artistic gesture is very much allied to modes of practice in the crafts. The flatness of the hand-drawn ellipse can be imagined in its original state on paper. Empathy with designers' ability to make the mark in the first place is a prerequisite of ownership of this kind of work. Functional considerations are, therefore, almost secondary.

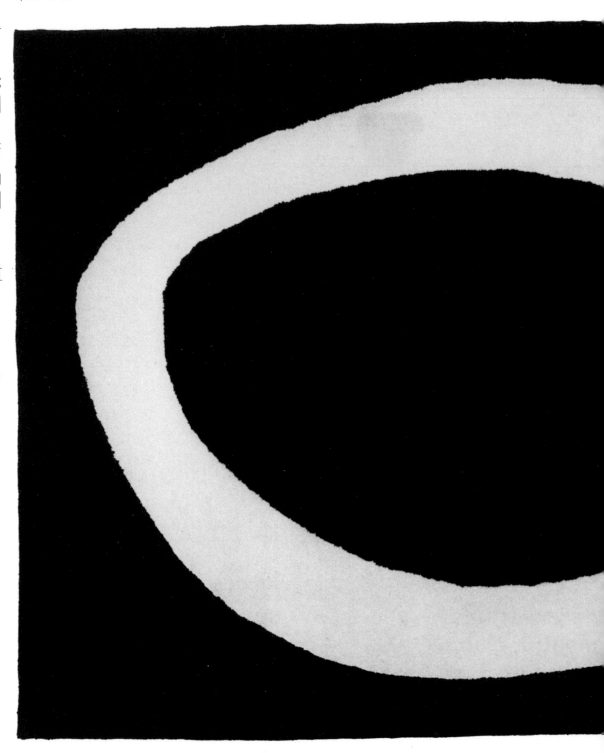

Javier Diez Blanco
Carpet – Vertigo
wool
w 240cm – l 170cm
w 94 1/2in – l 66 7/8in
Bd Ediciones de Diseño – Spain

Marcello Morandini
Handtufted Carpet — Proposta 7
wool
di 256cm
di 100 3/4in
Lantal Textiles — Switzerland

Handtufted Carpet — Proposta 8
wool
w 151cm — l 272cm
w 59 1/2in — l 107in
Lantal Textiles — Switzerland

The machinistic, op-art effect is counterbalanced by the handtufted production method. The time it takes to make these rugs almost defies their being trodden upon.

Handtufted Carpet – Proposta 2
wool
w 160cm – l 340cm
w 63in – l 133 7/8in
Lantal Textiles – Switzerland

Handtufted Carpet – Proposta 5
wool
w 100cm – l 300cm
w 39 3/8in – l 118in
Lantal Textiles – Switzerland

Feliksas Jakubauskas
Textile – Et Lux Aeterna Lucet ad Eis
wool – synthetics – Lurex
w 100cm – l 300cm
w 39 3/8in – l 118 1/8in
one-off

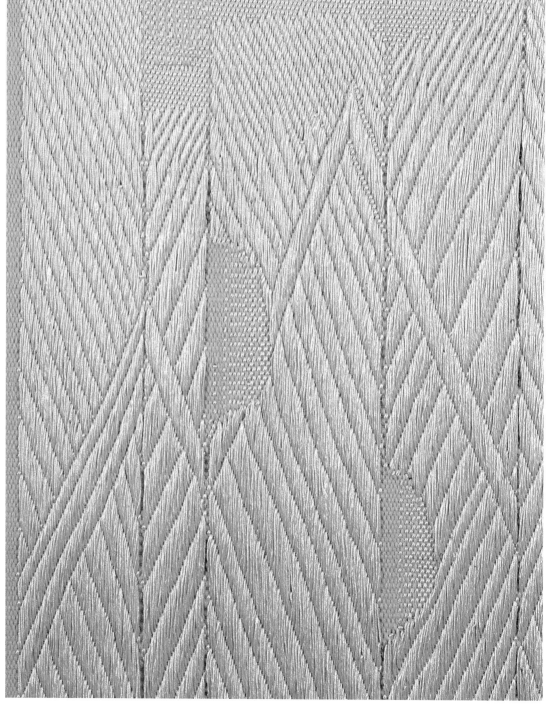

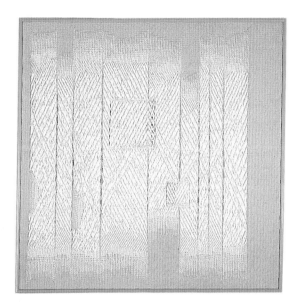
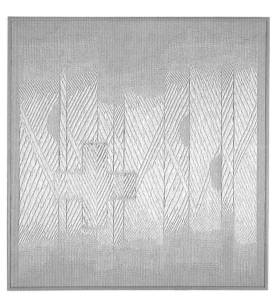

Feliksas Jakubauskas
Textile – Bleaching Sheets
wool – silk – synthetics
w 130cm – l 205cm
w 51 1/8in – l 80 3/4in
one-off

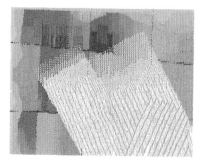

Christianna Los
Woven Tapestry – She-Shell
silk – linen
w 150cm – l 180cm – d 5cm
w 59in – l 70 7/8in – d 2in
Chris Los – UK
one-off

Ulf Moritz
Curtain — Nero
polyamide — polyester
w 138cm
w 54 1/4in
Sahco Hesslein — Germany

Ann Richards
Woven Scarf – Twill Pleat
silk
w 23cm – l 160cm
w 9in – l 63in
Whitchurch Silk Mill – UK
limited batch production

Hanna Korvela
Carpet – Duetto
w max. – 240cm
w max. – 94 1/4in
Adelta – Germany

Larsen Design – Dawn Hettrich
Various Textiles
Larsen – USA

Ann Richards
Woven Scarf – Spot Stripe
linen – silk
w 30cm – l 150cm
w 11 3/4in – l 59in
limited batch production

Vibeke Rohland
Textile – Abstract Archaeology
mercerized cotton – screenprint pigment
h (repeat) 80cm – w 140cm
h (repeat) 31 1/2in – w 55 1/8in
one-off

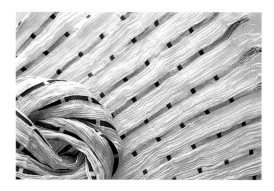

Jonas Bohlin
Carpet – Carpet on Carpet
wool
w 150cm – l 200cm
w 59in – l 78 3/4in
Asplund – Sweden

A pun.

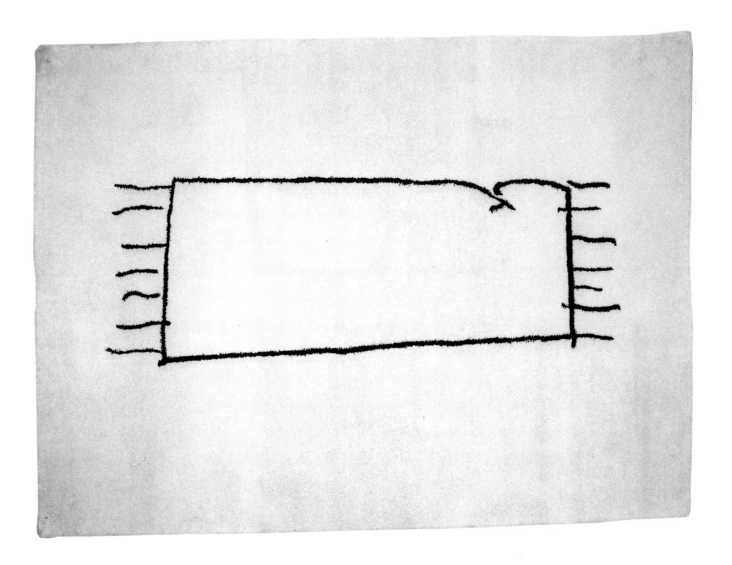

Carouschka Streiffert
Carpet
wool
w 200cm – l 200cm
w 78 3/4in – l 78 3/4in
Asplund – Sweden

Kurt Meinecke
Rug – Retro Series No. 27
wool
w 122cm – l 183cm
w 48in – l 72in
Meinecke Collection – USA

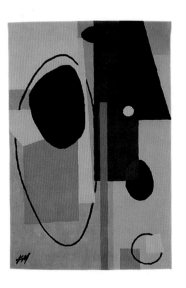

Christine Van der Hurd
Area Rug – Disco from Cuttin' a Rug collection
wool
w 152cm – l 213cm
w 60in – l 84in
limited batch production

"When I design carpets for a client's residence I try to convey warmth, ease and fun. I want the rugs to be danced on, walked on, played on, and to make people smile when they first see them."
– Christine Van der Hurd, USA

Biagio Cisotti and Sandra Laube
Carpet – Motion
wool
w 200cm – l 250cm
w 78 3/4in – l 98 3/8in
Namaste Handels – Germany

Kurt Meinecke
Rug – Karta Series No. 2
wool
w 122cm – l 183cm
w 48in – l 72in
Meinecke Collection – USA

Print Design YA/YA Inc.
Silkscreen Cotton – Gumbo Won
cotton
w 132cm
w 52in
YA/YA Young Aspirations/Young Artists – USA
limited batch production

Gerard Caliste
Hand-printed Fabric – Something's Fishy
cotton – silkscreen inks
w 38cm – l 81cm
w 15in – l 32in
YA/YA Young Aspirations/Young Artists – USA
sample piece

Gussena Martin
Textile
cotton – silkscreen inks
w 38cm – l 81cm
w 15in – l 32in
YA/YA Young Aspirations/Young Artists – USA
sample piece

Stojanka Strugar
Tapestry – One Summer Day
sisal
w 200cm – l 180cm
w 783/4in – l 707/8in
one-off

Stojanka Strugar
Tapestry – Composition
wool
w 160cm – l 120cm
w 63in – l 47 1/4in
one-off

Kurt Meinecke
Rug – Chicago Series No. 21
wool
w 122cm – l 183cm
w 48in – l 72in
Meinecke Collection – USA

Weyers and Borms
Carpet – Mouton Tourné
handtufted wool
w 230cm – l 370cm
w 90 1/2in – l 145 5/8in
Vera Vermeersch and Werner Gilson – Belgium
limited batch production

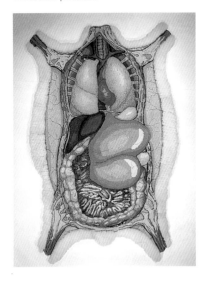

Renata Bonfanti
Tapestry – Algeria 25
wool – flax
h 162cm – w 90cm
h 63 3/4in – w 35 3/8in
Renata Bonfanti – Italy
limited production

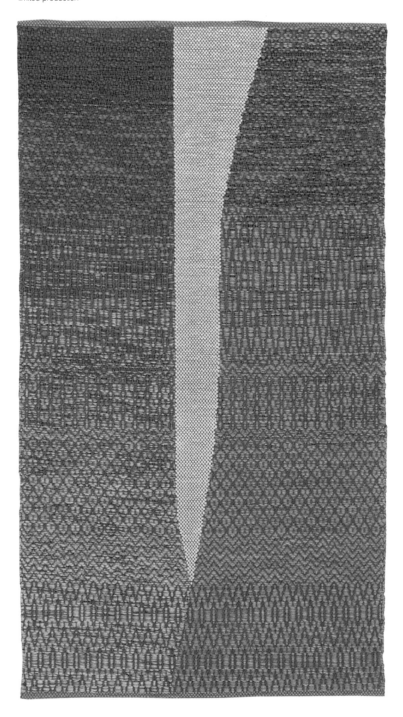

Sirkka Könönen
Carpet/wall hanging – Peacock I
jute
w 145cm – l 370cm
w 57in – l 145 5/8in
one-off

Vibeke Rohland
Textile – Juicy-Lucy
crêpe de chine
w 90cm – l 175cm
w 35 1/2in – l 68 7/8in
limited batch production

Dorte Østergaard Jakobsen
Textile — Float
cotton
w 130cm — l 550cm
w 51 1/8in — l 216 1/2in
Alive Design — Denmark
prototype

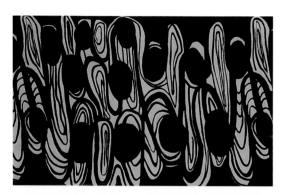

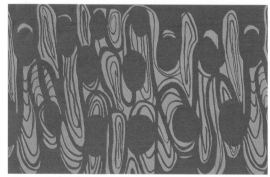

Nuala Goodman
Hand-painted Gown
silk satin — fabric paints
various sizes
Nuala Goodman — Italy
limited batch production

Sirkka Könönen
Carpet/Wall Hanging — Fairy Tale
wool — linen
h 150cm — w 110cm
h 59in — w 43 1/4in

Renata Bonfanti
Tapestry in Three Pieces – Gli Ecclesiasti
flax – wool – cotton
w 72cm – l 290cm
w 28 3/8in – l 114 1/8in
Renata Bonfanti – Italy
limited production

 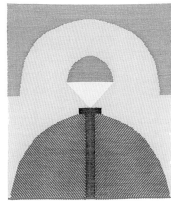 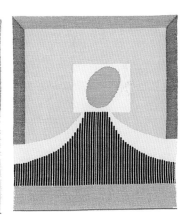

Products

Everything is a product.
Products are the carriers of the semantic signals of the consumer world.
Products function.
Products are transient symbols.
Products carry meaning and redefine domesticity.
Products are complex matrices of human invention.
No one person can repair a broken computer.
Electrical products which incorporate microchips are beyond the mechanical.
Machines no longer have to have moving parts to be called machines.
Products are status symbols.
Everything is a status symbol.

Roberto Pezzetta and
Zanussi Industrial Design Center
Washing Machine – Zoe
abs plastic
h 85cm – w 60cm – d 55cm
h 33 1/2in – w 23 5/8in – d 21 5/8in
Electrolux Zanussi – Italy

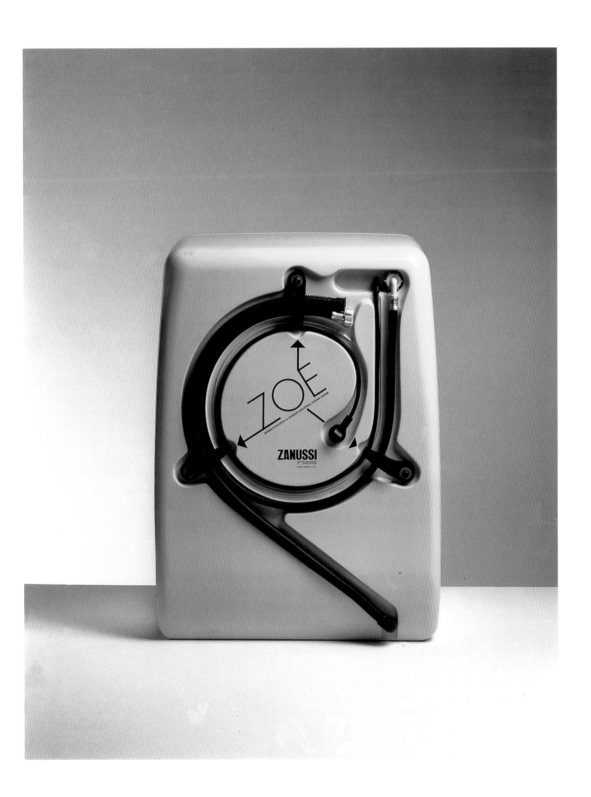

Kaoru Sumita
Digital Still Camera – DSC-F1
compressed aluminium
h 7.8cm – w 10.2cm – d 4cm
h 3in – w 4in – d 1 5/8in
Sony Corp. – Japan

Kaoru Sumita
Digital Video Camera – DCR-PC7
die-cast magnesium
h 12.9cm – w 5.9cm – d 11.8cm
h 5in – w 2 3/8in – d 4 3/4in
Sony Corp. – Japan

JVC Design Centre
Digital Video Camera with LCD Monitor – GR-DVM1D
aluminium – plastics
h 15.6cm – w 6cm – d 9.4cm
h 6 1/8in – w 2 3/8in – d 3 5/8in
JVC – Japan

The advent of the DVC has the potential to transform the language of television. Small cameras that can deliver near broadcast quality with AVID compatibility effectively remove the need for some of the rigmarole of film making. Some feature films are being shot using these small cameras, and this technology, although in its relative infancy, has the potential to have the same effect on film making as sampling technology has had on music.

Yoshifumi Ishikawa
Camera – Canon IXUS Z90
aluminium – abs
h 6.5cm – w 12cm – d 5cm
h 2 1/2in – w 4 3/4in – d 2in
Design Centre – Canon Inc. – Japan

Hiroyuki Kimura
Autofocus Single-Lens Reflex Camera – Canon EOS 1X
stainless steel – abs
h 8cm – w 13cm – d 6cm
h 3 1/8in – w 5 3/8in – d 2 3/8in
Design Centre – Canon Inc. – Japan

Yasushi Shiotani
Camera – Canon IXUS IX 240
stainless steel – pc – abs
h 6cm – w 9cm – d 2.7cm
h 2 3/8in – w 3 1/2in – d 1in
Design Centre – Canon Inc. – Japan

The stylish and automated pocket camera with a good lens.

Olympus
Camera – Centurion
polycarbonite – rubber
h 8.3cm – w 11.8cm – d 11.1cm
h 3 1/4in – w 4 5/8in – d 4 3/8in
Olympus Optical Co. (Europa) GmbH – Germany

Volkswagen AG
Compact Binoculars
abs – rubber
h 10cm – w 6cm – d 4cm
h 3 7/8in – w 2 3/8in – d 1 1/2in
Minox – Germany

Herbst LaZar Bell Inc. – Mark Dziersk
Document Shredder – The Shark
polystyrene
h 4cm – l 14cm – d 36cm
h 1 3/4in – l 5 1/2in – d 14in
General Binding Corporation – USA

Hector Santos
Single Page Scanner – PET (Personal Enhancement Tool)
abs – stainless steel
h 10cm – w 30cm – d 7.6cm
h 4in – w 11 3/4in – d 3in
prototype

Michele de Lucchi and Johannes Kiessler
Ink-Jet Printer – JP 790
plastic
h 46cm – l 38cm – d 16cm
h 18 1/8in – l 15in – d 6 1/4in
Olivetti Lexikon – Italy

Tetsuya Sekine
Colour Bubble-Jet Printer – Canon BJC-4200
abs
h 20cm – w 38cm – d 23cm
h 7 7/8in – w 15in – d 9in
Design Centre – Canon Inc. – Japan

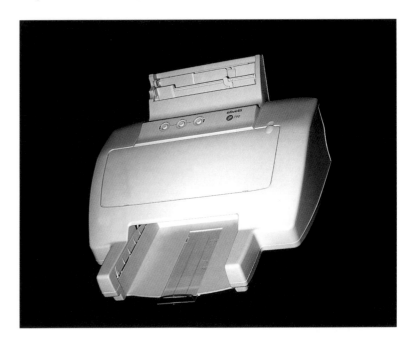

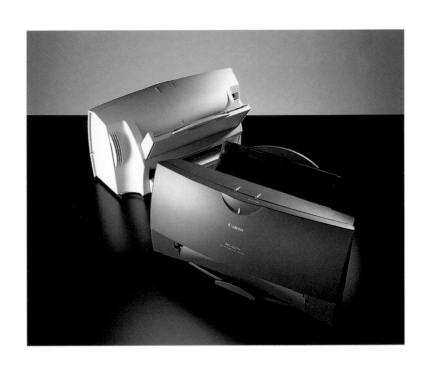

Shinkichi Tanaka
Attaché Case – Expert II LA-615C – LA-610
aluminium
h 31cm – w 42cm – d 9cm/7cm
h 12 1/4in – w 16 1/2in – d 3 1/2in/2 3/4in
Fujikowa Industry Co. – Japan

Steve Jones and Samson Christofides – DPG
Computer Under Desk Sling
powder-coated steel – polypropylene
w 15cm – l 60cm
w 5 7/8in – l 23 5/8in
DPG – UK

Yamaha Product Design Laboratory
Music Data Player – MDP 10
abs – fabric
h 17cm – w 39cm – d 20cm
h 6 5/8in – w 23 1/4in – d 7 7/8in
Yamaha Corporation – Japan

Yamaha Product Design Laboratory
Divided Pickup for Guitar – G1D
abs
h 3cm – w 8.5cm – d 7.5cm
h 1 1/8in – w 3 1/4in – d 2 7/8in
Yamaha Corporation – Japan

Andy Davey
Clockwork Radio – Freeplay
abs
h 20cm – w 31cm – d 10cm
h 7 7/8in – w 12 1/4in – d 3 7/8in
BayGen Power Europe – UK

Matsushita Electric Industrial Co. Ltd
Portable CD Tuner System – SL-PH7
abs – aluminium
h 18cm – w 46cm – d 7cm
h 7in – w 18 1/8in – d 2 3/4in
Matsushita Electric Industrial Co. – Japan

Yamaha Product Design Laboratory
Digital Drum – DD-50
abs
h 14cm – w 55cm – d 35cm
h 5 1/2in – w 21 5/8in – d 13 3/4in
Yamaha Corporation – Japan

Daisuke Ishii and Takahiro Tsuge
Portable MiniDisc Player – MZ-E50
die-cast magnesium
h 1.4cm – w 9.9cm – d 7.4cm
h 1/2in – w 3 7/8in – d 2 7/8in
Sony Corp. – Japan

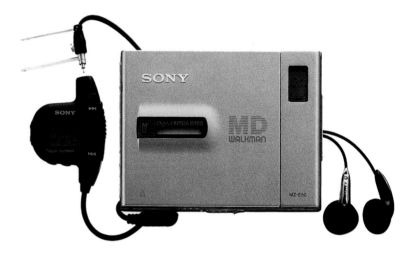

The Sony MiniDisc is seen by some as yet another format buster, which has its own set of hardware and yet further chain of upgrades for the hapless consumer to buy into. The digital revolution is inherent in this product. Personal soundtracks moved around and composed with no deterioration in quality.

Joe Tan
Speakerphone – Soundpoint
injection moulded ABS
h 7cm – di 17.5cm
h 2 3/4in – di 6 7/8in
Polycom – USA

Peter Kunz
CD Holder – A.B.CD
stainless steel – plastic
h 30cm – w 12cm – l 90cm
h 11 3/4in – w 4 3/4in – l 35 3/8in
Robots – Italy

Piero Polato
CD Holder – Studium CD 7-14-21
aluminium – anodized silver
h 0.7cm – w 12cm – d 43cm/29cm/14cm
h 1/4in – w 43/4in – d 167/8in/113/8in/51/2in
Nava Design – Italy

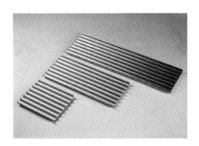

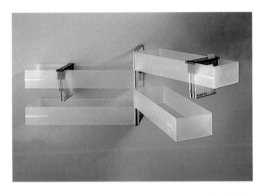

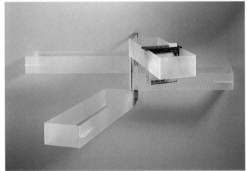

Yuji Morimiya
25" Colour TV – Plasmatron PZ-2500
plastic – net
h 48cm – w 84cm – d 24.2cm
h 18 7/8in – w 33in – d 9 1/2in
Sony Corp. – Japan

The plasma screen widescreen TV is the latest addition to the armoury of home entertainment. The notion of home cinema for all those interested is not so far away with the introduction of this technology. The plasma screen has luminosity akin to a cinema screen, as opposed to the harsh radiation from behind glass of the conventional cathode-ray tube.

Arnout Visser – Peter van der Jagt and Erik-Jan Kwakkel
Function Tiles – DMD45
ceramic
h 15cm – w 15cm
h 5 7/8in – w 5 7/8in
DMD – The Netherlands

Saar Oosterhof
Soft Tiles – DD79
soft polyurethane
h 24cm – w 24cm – d 1.4cm
h 9 3/8in – w 9 3/8in – d 5/8in
prototype
DMD – The Netherlands

Droog Design have been carving a niche as the publisher of a number of products conceived with wit and dryness by a loosely affiliated coterie of Dutch designers. Working independently of each other, the designers manage to coagulate around the Droog idea. Noted for their consistent stream of strange, yet functional, narrative executions.

"Original ideas, clear concepts designed in a dry, that is, sober fashion."
— Droog Design, The Netherlands.

Marco Susani and Mario Trimarchi
Travel Trays – Flat
polypropylene
h 8cm – w 25cm – l 33cm
h 3 1/8in – w 9 7/8in – l 13in
Serafino Zani – Italy

Mikala Naur
Kitchen-Roll Holder – Roll-X
recyclable polypropylene
h 11.5cm – w 11.5cm – l 24cm
h 4 1/2in – w 4 1/2in – l 9 3/8in
prototype

Enzo Mari
Learning Game – 16 Animals
expanded polystyrene
h 3.5cm – w 25.5cm – l 35.5cm
h 1 3/8in – w 10in – l 14in
Alessi – Italy

Winfried Scheuer
Laundry Basket – Ero
plastic – polypropylene
h 67cm – w 25cm – d 38cm
h 26 3/8in – w 9 7/8in – d 15in
Zaket – Germany

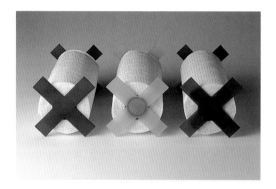

Alejandro Ruiz
Flower Pot – Twilight
recyclable polypropylene
h 18cm – di 21cm
h 7in – di 8 1/4in
Authentics – Germany

Anonymous Design from the 1970s
Folding Watering Can
vinyl
w 26cm – l 36cm
w 10 1/4in – l 14 1/8in
Di(Sain) – Austria

Julian Brown
Beverage Can Compactor – Attila
engineering polymer
h 38.5cm – d 12cm
h 15 1/8in – d 4 3/4in
Rexite – Italy

Julian Brown
Plastic Bottle Compactor – Cricket
polypropylene – steel
h 74cm – di 16.5cm
h 29 1/8in – di 6 1/2in
Rexite – Italy

Toshiba Corporation Design Centre
Compact Vacuum Cleaner – VC Z3L
plastics – metals
h 18cm – w 12cm – d 23cm
h 7in – w 4 3/4in – d 9in
Toshiba Corporation – Japan

Winfried Scheuer
Door Wedge – James
TPE
h 2cm – w 6cm – l 18cm
h 3/4in – w 2 3/8in – l 7in
Helix-Akantus – Germany

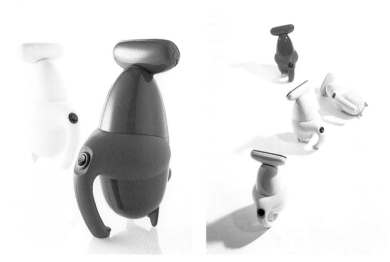

"We don't consider product design as simply a way
to 'dress up' our technology. The form of a product
should bring a sense of aesthetic fulfilment to the user.
The design of electrical products should not only be
functional but also provide a service when not being
used, that is the product should have an appearance
that pleases people."
– Design Centre, Toshiba Corporation, Japan

Hans Maier-Aichen
Wastepaper Basket – Cap
recyclable polypropylene
h 39cm – di 30.5cm
h 15 3/8in – di 12in
Authentics – Germany

Mats Theselius
Tumbler – Victoria
recyclable polypropylene
h 12.4cm – d 8cm
h 4 7/8in – d 3 1/8in
Authentics – Germany

Hans Maier-Aichen
Bottle Basket – 6 Times
recyclable polypropylene
h 32.5cm – w 33.5cm – d 22cm
h 12 3/4in – w 13 1/8in – d 8 5/8in
Authentics – Germany

The idea behind the Authentics range is to explore
and express the nature of the polypropylene from
which most if not all of their products seem to be
made. Authenticity is delivered by dint of the fact that
Aichen and cohorts rarely stray from their engaging
and well thought-out path.

Winfried Scheuer
Newspaper Holder – News
plastic – polypropylene
h 36cm – w 22cm – d 35cm
h 14 1/8in – w 8 5/8in – d 13 3/4in
Zaket – Germany

Karim Rashid
Wastepaper Basket – Garbo
injection moulded high-impact polypropylene
h 43cm – w 34cm – l 33cm
h 17in – w 13 1/2in – l 13in
Umbra – Canada

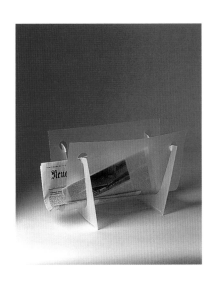

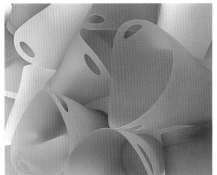

Philippe Starck
Radio with Automatic Search Facility – Poe
coloured polystyrene
h 24.5cm – w 18cm – l 16.5cm
h 9 5/8in – w 7in – l 6 1/2in
Alessi – Italy

Laurence and Constantin Boym
Kitchen Utensils – Spaghetti
recyclable polypropylene – polyamide
spatula – h 3cm – w 7cm – l 35cm
          h 1 1/8in – w 2 3/4in – l 13 3/4in
ladle – h 7.5cm – w 7.5cm – l 31cm
          h 2 7/8in – w 2 7/8in – l 12 1/4in
spaghetti tongs – h 4cm – w 7cm – l 34cm
          h 1 5/8in – w 2 3/4in – l 13 3/8in
Authentics – Germany

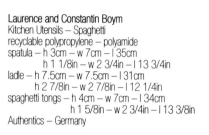

Enzo Mari
Desk Accessories – Manhattan
technopolymer – steel
3 trays – h 17.5cm – w 75cm – d 33cm
          h 6 7/8in – w 29 1/2in – d 13in
Alias – Italy

Marco Ferreri
Vase Holder on Wheels – Riomaggiore
chromed steel – plastic
h 34cm/14cm – w 68cm/35cm – l 80cm
h 13 3/8in/5 1/2in – w 26 3/4in/13 3/4in – l 31 1/2in
Robots – Italy

Geoff Hollington
Pens and Pencils – Frontier
abs plastic – stainless steel
l 14cm – di 1cm
l 5 1/2in – di 3/8in
Parker Pen Company –
Gilette Stationery Products Group – UK

Stefan Patte
Picture Frame – Magnum
magnets – stainless steel – glass
h 25.5cm – w 18cm – d 8cm
h 10in – w 7in – d 3 1/8in
D. Slapansky – S. Patte Design – Germany
limited batch production

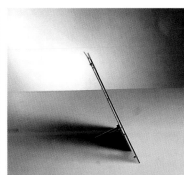

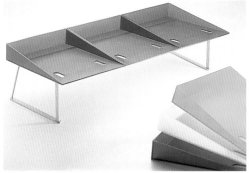

Oscar Tusquets and Lluís Clotet
Extractor – Campana Diafana
perspex – aluminium – oil-resistant nitrilic rubber
h 35cm – w 50cm – d 90cm
h 13 3/4in – w 19 5/8in – d 35 3/8in
Bd Ediciones de Diseño – Spain

Donato D'Urbino and Paolo Lomazzi – DDL Studio
Coathanger – Appendinuvole
steel
h 165cm – di 60cm
h 65in – di 23 5/8in
Naos LaCasaAnimata – Italy

Karim Rashid
Clock – Gyro
spun aluminium – chrome
di 15cm
di 5 7/8in
Umbra – Canada

Alfredo Häberli and Christophe Marchand
Adjustable Book-Ends – Pinocchio
pearwood – solid wood
h 25–42cm
h 9 7/8–16 1/2in
Alias – Italy

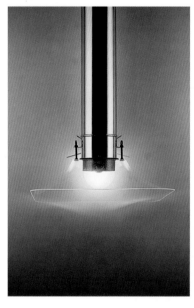

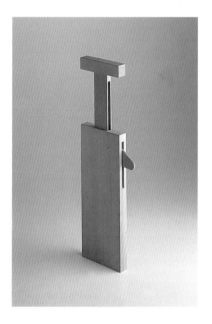
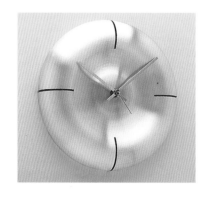

Makio Hasuike
Door Handle – Edo
brass – matt chrome finish
l 13.7cm – d 6.7cm
l 5 3/8in – d 2 5/8in
Colombo Design – Italy

Bonini Spicciolato
Door Handle – Ludus
brass – cast polyester resin
h 3cm – w 5cm – d 3cm
h 1 1/8in – w 2in – d 1 1/8in
Colombo Design – Italy

Foster and Partners
Door Handle
stainless steel – wood – various metals
various sizes
Valli and Valli – Italy

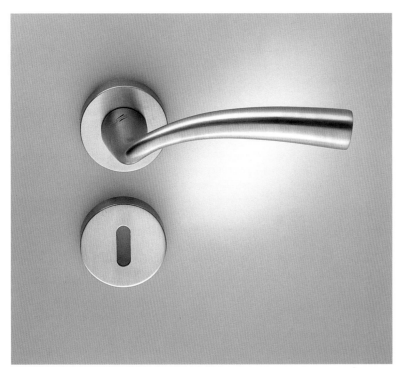

Jonathan Marshall
Stamp Scale
stainless steel
w 5.5cm – l 8.5cm – d 0.3cm
w 2 1/8in – l 3 3/8in – d 1/8in
prototype

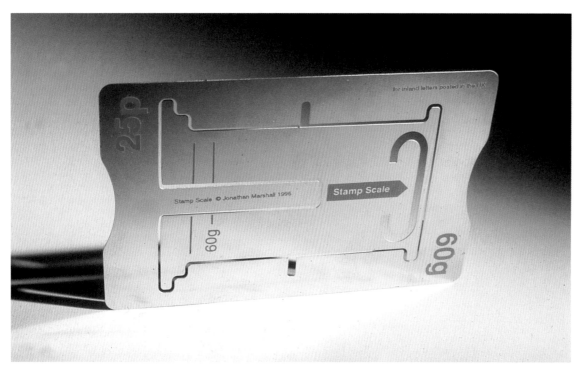

Jean Nouvel
Computer Support – Less
solid core laminate – aluminium
h 138cm/122cm – w 56cm – d 38cm
h 54 3/8in/48in – w 22in – d 15in
Unifor SpA – Italy

Knud Holscher
Sound Screening
extruded aluminium – laminated hardened glass
h 240–350cm
h 94 1/2–137 3/4in
Aluplus – Denmark

Daniel Gilgen and Rolf Degel
Didactic Toy – Solar-mobile
foam rubber
h 8cm – w 8cm – l 12cm
h 3 1/8in – w 3 1/8in – l 4 3/4in
U-X – Germany
limited batch production

The sound screen may be pushing the boundaries of the domestic, but in that it is erected against noise blight it is defining and protecting the domestic environment from intrusion. A domestic boundary in aluminium and glass.

Knud Holscher
Elements for Blind People – Pictoform
cast iron
module – h 10cm – w 10cm – l 30cm
         h 3 7/8in – w 3 7/8in – l 11 3/4in
GH Form – Denmark

Knud Holscher
Numerals + Letters
stainless steel
h 15cm – d 1.2cm
h 5 7/8in – d 1/2in
D Line International – Denmark

Marian de Rond and Terri Pecora
Cushion – Play Cushion
cotton – foam – nylon
h 12cm – l 65cm – d 65cm
h 4 3/4in – l 25 5/8in – d 25 5/8in
T. P. Rond – Italy

Play Rug
nylon – cotton – Dacron
w 130cm – l 130cm
w 51 1/8in – l 51 1/8in
T. P. Rond – Italy

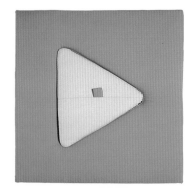

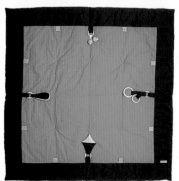

Baby Bag for Push Chair – Sleeping Bag
nylon – cotton – Dacron
h 89cm – w 46cm
h 35in – w 18 1/8in
T. P. Rond – Italy

Leif Hagerup
Cycle Trailer – Dolphin
aluminium – polyurethane – impact-resitant polyethylene – pvc-free nylon
h 90cm – w 79cm – l 162cm
h 35 3/8in – w 31 1/8in – l 63 3/4in
A. Winther – Denmark

Stefan Lippert and Michael Krohn – Industrial
Wheelchair – Jet
aluminium
h 80cm – w 55cm – d 80cm
h 31 1/2in – w 21 5/8in – d 31 1/2in
Proactiv – Germany

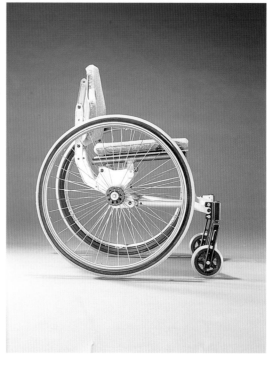

Arguably, for a child the domestic arena extends to wherever their parents take them. In this case home is the three wheeled cycle trolley. Not advisable on city roads in the rain or the rush hour.

Mike Holroyd
Breath-Operated Inhaler – Easi-Breathe
filled polypropylene
h 10cm – di 3.5cm
h 3 7/8in – di 1 3/8in
Norton Healthcare – UK

Gerald Wurz
Screen System – X-In Balance
balloon silk – stainless steel
h 300cm/240cm/220cm – w 160cm/120cm/80cm
h 118 1/8in/94 1/2in/86 5/8in – w 63in/47 1/4in/31 1/2in
Nova Form – Austria

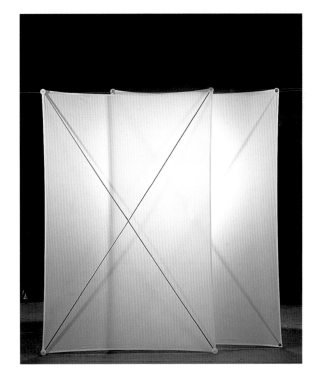

"To make a simple product doesn't imply that a product is a simple thing to make."
– Gerald Wurz, Germany

Paul Priestman
Radiator – Hot Springs
steel
h 180cm/120cm/60cm
h 70 7/8in/47 1/4in/23 5/8in
Bisque – UK

Patrizio Roffi
Snowboard – X-Type 152
carbon – fibreglass – wood – rubber –
steel – epoxy
h 28cm – w 25cm – l 152cm
h 11in – w 9 7/8in – l 59 7/8in
DNR Sportsystem – Switzerland

Thomas Zawalski
Spirit Level – Delphin
aluminium
h 3cm – w 0.5cm – l 15cm
h 1 1/8in – w 1/8in – l 5 7/8in
Zaket – Germany

N/P/K Industrial Design
Set of Tyre Levers
glass fibre reinforced polyamide
h 2cm – w 1.5cm – l 11.5cm
h 3/4in – w 5/8in – l 4 1/2in
Technische Industrie Tacx – The Netherlands

Feldmann + Schultchen
Folding Hand Cart – Kango
fibre-reinforced plastic – cordura
h 85cm – w 25cm – l 70cm
h 33 1/2in – w 9 7/8in – l 27 1/2in
Feldmann + Schultchen – Germany
patented prototype for mass production

  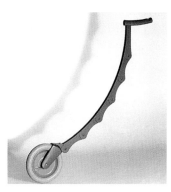 

Ducati
Monster M900
engine type – 900cc – four stroke twin cylinder
max. power – 66.6 HP at 7000 rpm
Ducati – Italy

Robbiano Design
Bimota 500 V due
engine type – 500cc – two stroke twin cylinder
max. power – 110 HP at 9000 rpm
Bimota – Italy

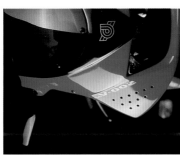

Ferrari 550 Maranello
engine type – V12
best performer 0–60 – 4.3 seconds
max. speed – 200 mph
drive system – rear wheel
Ferrari – Italy

Fiat Coupé (2 models)
engine type – 5 cylinder
best performer 0–60 – 6.4 seconds
max. speed – 150 mph
drive system – front wheel
Fiat – Italy

The car is an extension of the home.

Alfa Romeo 156
engine type – 4 cylinder
best performer 0–62 – 8.6 seconds
max. speed – 134 mph
drive system – front wheel
Alfa Romeo – Italy

SLK Roadster (2 models)
engine type – 4 cylinder
best performer 0–60 – 7.6 seconds
max. speed – 150 mph
drive system – rear wheel
Daimler Benz – Germany

Audi A6 (23 models)
engine type – 4 cylinder – 5 cylinder or V6
best performer 0–60 – 6.8 seconds
max. speed – 150 mph
drive system– front wheel or four wheel
Audi – Germany

Volkswagen Passat (15models)
engine type – 4 cylinder or 2xV6
best performer 0–60 – 8.7 seconds
max. speed – 140 mph
drive system – front wheel
Volkswagen – Germany

Ford Ka (2 models)
engine type – 4 cylinder
best performer 0–60 – 14 seconds
max. speed – 95 mph
drive system – front wheel
Ford – UK

Biographies
Suppliers
Acquisitions
Photographic Credits

Carina Andersson was born in Stockholm in 1965. She studied glass and ceramic design and has exhbited her work throughout Scandinavia and at the Milan Triennale (1994); the 'Not so Simple' show in New York (1996); and the Victoria and Albert Museum, London (1997). – 109

Andrea Anselmi and Corrado Baglioni studied at the Polytechnic School of Design in Milan and the Istituto Europeo di Disegno, respectively. They worked for various architectural and design firms before starting their collaboration. They won the Young Designers Award in 1993 and the Osram competition in 1996. – 95

Ron Arad was born in Tel Aviv in 1951. He studied at the Jerusalem Academy of Art, and from 1974–79 at the Architectural Association, London, where he was taught by Peter Cook and Bernhard Tschumi. In 1981 he founded One Off Ltd with Caroline Thorman and in 1983 designed One Off's first showroom in Neal Street, Covent Garden. Well-known early pieces include the Rover Chair, the vacuum-packed Transformer Chair and the remote-controlled Aerial Light. Later work explored the use of tempered steel first in the Well-Tempered Chair and later in the Bookworm. In 1988 Arad won the Tel Aviv Opera Foyer Interior Competition with C. Norton and S. McAdam, and the next year formed Ron Arad Associates with Caroline Thorman and Alison Brooks in order to realize the project, moving the firm's premises to Chalk Farm, London. As well as the design and construction of the new One Off Design Studio, furniture gallery and workshop in 1990, recent projects have included furniture design for Poltronova, Vitra, Moroso and Driade; the design of various interior installations; the design of the restaurants Belgo and Belgo Centrale in London; domestic architectural projects; and the Adidas Stadium, the flagship complex in Paris. In 1994 Arad established the Ron Arad Studio in Como to continue and expand on the production of limited-edition, handmade pieces. Arad was a guest professor at the Hochschule in Vienna from 1994–97 and is currently Professor of Furniture Design at the Royal College of Art in London. – 39

Sigeaki Asahara was born in Tokyo in 1948 and studied in Turin, Italy. Since 1973 he has worked as a freelance industrial designer in Tokyo. He exhibits internationally, and one of his projects is on permanent show at the Brooklyn Museum of New York. His work has received much acclaim including the IF Best of Category Award, Hanover, in 1992. – 84, 90–91, 93

Teppo Asikainen see Valvomo Ltd

Sergio Asti was born in Milan in 1926. He graduated in architecture from Milan Polytechnic and set up his own studio in 1953. He was one of the founding members of the ADI (Associazione per Il Disegno Industriale) and is still an honorary member. He designs furniture, lighting, glassware, wooden products, ceramics, electrical appliances, interiors, stores and exhibitions. He has received numerous awards including the gold medal at the XI Milan Triennale and a Compasso d'Oro (1962), and his work has been exhibited internationally. Asti has served on juries for architecture and industrial design competitions, and has given lectures both in Italy and abroad. – 79, 130

Masayo Ave was born in Tokyo in 1962. She graduated from the architectural department at Hosei University, and after working in the architectural office of Ichiro Ebihara, moved to Milan and completed her Masters degree in industrial design at the Domus Academy. She established her own design studio, Ave Design Co., in 1992, and since then has received international acclaim for her works in the fields of industrial, furniture and textile design, theatre sets and architecture. She is particularly interested in the potential of new materials such as the Shibori textile, and in the fusion of traditional Japanese tie-dyeing techniques with modern technology. – 78

Shin and Tomoko Azumi studied industrial design at Kyoto City University of Art and the Royal College of Art, London. In 1996 they were finalists in the Blueprint/100% Design Awards. They founded Azumi's in 1995, undertaking projects for British, Italian and Japanese clients. They have exhibited at Sotheby's and at the Crafts Council in London. – 56, 83

Grazia Azzolin was born in Treviso, Italy, in 1961. She studied medicine before attending the industrial design school in Padua in 1992. She has worked as art director for an architectural studio in Castelfranco and has developed designs for companies such as Benetton (glasses), Panto (a wooden door) and Olivari (a door handle). – 87

Corrado Baglioni see Andrea Anselmi

Mario Barbaglia and Marco Colombo have been working together since 1975, specializing in interior design. In 1984 they expanded their design work to include some industrial products, collaborating with PAF (now Italiana Luce) and substantially changing its image. Their work has received worldwide acclaim. – 102

Jakob Berg graduated from the Royal Danish Arts Academy in 1987. He has worked for a number of design practices and furniture companies and has exhibited his work in Denmark and abroad. His work is represented in the Danish Museum for Arts and Crafts in Copenhagen. – 52

Tom Bisig and Nicole Naas were born in Switzerland in 1964 and 1968, respectively. They studied at the Höheren Schule für Gestaltung in Basle and began their collaboration in 1993, forming their own design practice, Naas and Bisig. – 54

Julie Blyfield trained as a jewellery designer and for ten years was a partner in a contemporary jewellery cooperative. For the past seven years she has worked on larger scale work and architectural commissions, designing exterior screens, fences, signage panels and counters. In 1995 she won the Sir Zelman Cowan Award from the Australian Institute of Architects for the Swallowcliffe School Project. – 111

Jonas Bohlin studied interior design at National College of Art, Craft and Design in Stockholm from 1977–81. At present he lectures at the Beckmans School of Design where he started the furniture design programme in 1991. Projects include the Concrete chair, Slottsbacken cupboard and the Spring iron sofa. His work can be seen in Röhss Museum of Arts and Crafts in Gothenburg, the Malmö Art Museum and the Danish Museum of Decorative Art in Copenhagen. – 157

Renata Bonfanti was educated at the Istituto Statale d'Arte in Venice and at the Kvinnelige Industriskole in Oslo in the early 1950s. She produces hand-woven rugs and tapestries as well as machine-woven material. She has taken part in numerous exhibitions and competitions, including the Milan Triennale (1954, '57, '60, '64), the Venice Biennale (1956–60), the Biennale de la Tapisserie, Lausanne (1975–77) and the 'Design since 1945' exhibition at the Philadelphia Museum of Art (1983). In 1962 she received the Compasso d'Oro. – 164, 169

Jörg Boner was born in Uster, in 1968. He served an apprenticeship as a joiner and draughtsman and worked as a freelance builder until 1992 when he began studies in interior and product design at the School of Arts in Basle. – 63

Santina Bonini and Ernesto Spicciolato founded their product design office in Milan in 1990. They are also involved in the development of interior design projects for commercial spaces, booths for trade shows and small-scale architectural schemes. Santina Bonini worked with Andrea Branzi until 1991 on, amongst other projects, the New Contemporary Art Museum in Arezzo. She studied architecture in Florence and was a founder member of DIN, Industrial Design Consulting (1992). Ernesto Spicciolato also studied architecture in Florence. He founded Elettra (1982), Bolidismo (1985) and DIN (1992). From 1987–90 he worked with Makio Hasuike before starting his collaboration with Bonini. Bonini and Spicciolato have exhibited their work internationally, most recently in the New York Museum of Modern Art's show 'Mutant Materials in Contemporary Design' (1995). The drawings which won Spicciolato second place in fthe New York Waterfront Competition can be seen in the Pompidou Collection in Paris. Clients include Alessi, Cappellini, Colombo Design, Domus Design Agency, Sedie and Company and Unitalia. – 201

Constantin Boym was born in Moscow in 1955. He graduated from the Moscow Architectural Institute in 1978 and from 1984–85 studied for a Masters degree in design at the Domus Academy in Milan. He became a registered architect in the USA in 1988 and today has his own design consultancy in New York. He has designed award-winning products for many international companies including Morphos, Néotù and the Formica Corporation. Since 1986 he has taught at the Parsons School of Design, New York, where he currently serves as a director of product studies in the Department of Product Design. Awards include the ID Annual Design Award (1988 and 1990). His work is included in the permanent collections of the Cooper-Hewitt Museum, New York, and the Musée des Arts Décoratifs in Montreal. – 198

David Braun was born in Lucerne, Switzerland, in 1965. He studied product and interior design as well as architecture and taught himself CAD graphic layout and image processing. He worked as a freelance designer in Berlin before starting his collaboration with N2 in 1997, and is also involved in graphic design, image processing and multimedia projects. – 62

Julian Brown was born in Northampton, UK, in 1955. He graduated from the Royal College of Art in London and completed his training by working for a leading design studio in Austria. He has since designed for many international companies and has a long-standing connection with the Hochschule der Künste in Berlin where he was a guest professor in 1992. – 194

Antoine Cahen graduated in industrial design from the Lausanne Art School in 1975. He worked as a freelance designer before setting up Les Ateliers du Nord in 1983 with his partners, industrial designer Claude Frossard and graphic designer Werner Jeker. His activities include the study and development of products and equipment in fields as varied as transport, museography and domestic applicances, as well as the creation of his own products. – 95

Gerard Caliste was born in the United States in 1979 and was a student designer with YA/YA Design in New Orleans. He currently attends the L.E. Rabouin Career Magnet High School. He has designed for the United Nations 50th Anniversary in conjunction with Swatch, and his work has been exhibited throughout the USA. – 161

Caroline Casey has a degree in fashion and textile design and ran her own clothing business before moving to New York to study interior design at the Parsons School of Design. Whilst in the United States she received the Palazzetti Prize which, upon her return to Australia, led to her first solo show. Her work can be seen in the Australian National Gallery, Canberra, and the San Francisco Museum of Modern Art. A new collection will form the content of a solo exhibition at the Powerhouse Museum in Sydney in 1998. – 63

Achille Castiglioni, born in Milan in 1918, began his career immediately after the Second World War with his brothers Livio and Pier Giacomo. He is well known for his innovative designs in interiors, furniture and lighting, and his clients include Flos, Phonola, Bernini, Cassina, de Padova, Fontana Arte, Interflex, Kartell, Marcatré, Olivetti, Up & Up and Zanotta. Castiglioni is one of the foremost talents in Italian design and has been honoured nine times with the Compasso d'Oro. His work is in the collections of the Victoria and Albert Museum, London; the Museum of Modern Art, New York; the Israel Museum, Jerusalem; and in museums in Prague, Zurich, Munich, Düsseldorf, Cologne, Hamburg and Helsinki. He is currently Professor of Industrial Design and Decoration at the University of Milan. – 81, 118, 123, 139, 141

Samson Christofides founded DPG in 1993 to create design-led products for the contract furniture and domestic markets. Since then the company has produced desking, office accessories and lighting and is currently working on its first seating programme. – 181

Biagio Cisotti and Sandra Laube have been working together since 1993. Cisotti was born in Aradeo, Italy, in 1955 and graduated in architecture from Florence University in 1980 where he also taught from 1981–92. In 1982 he started his collaboration with Poltronova, becoming ardirector. Since 1989 he has lectured at ISIA (the Istituto Superiore delle Industrie Artistiche) and worked with Aurea, a design and architecture studio in Munich. He was also responsible for the conception and development of B.R.F. He has exhibited his work throughout Europe. Sandra Laube studied at ISIA, graduating in 1983. In 1992 she was awarded a scholarship from the College of Art and Design, Minneapolis. She is at present working in graphics and has participated in various exhibitions, holding a solo show in 1996 in Rottweil, Germany. – 160

Antonio Citterio was born in Meda, Italy, in 1950, and has been involved in industrial and furniture design since 1967. He studied at Milan Polytechnic and in 1973 set up a studio with Paolo Nava. The two have worked jointly and individually for B & B Italia and Flexform, among other clients. In 1979 they were awarded the Compasso d'Oro. In 1987 Terry Dwan became a partner in Studio Citterio Dwan, and the company has undertaken many interior design projects since then, including a range of schemes for Esprit and offices and showrooms for Vitra. Among the work realized in Japan, in partnership with Toshiyuki Kita, is the headquarters in Kobe for World Company; the Corrente Building in Tokyo; and, in 1992, the Daigo headquarters in Tokyo. Citterio has taught at the Domus Academy in Milan and has participated in many exhibitions, including independent shows in Hanover, Rome, Amsterdam, Paris and Weil. In 1993 he designed the layout of the exhibition 'Antonio Citterio and Terry Dwan' promoted by Arc en Rêve in Bordeaux, which travelled to both Osaka and Tokyo in 1994. – 44

Lluis Clotet was born in Barcelona in 1941, and in 1965 graduated from the Escuela Técnica de Arquitectura in Barcelona. In 1964 he founded Studio Per with the architects Pep Bonet, Christian Cirici and Oscar Tusquets and has collaborated on numerous projects with them. He is a founder member of Bd Ediciones de Diseño, for which he still designs furniture and objects. He received the FAD award for the best interior in Barcelona in 1965 and 1972. He has also received the Delta de Oro on three occasions for his industrial design. – 200

Marco Colombo see Mario Barbaglia

Nick Crosbie was born in 1971. He has a degree in industrial design from Central Saint Martin's College of Art and Design and a Masters degree from the Royal College of Art, London. He set up Inflate in 1995. – 132–3

Andy Davey is principal of TKO Product Design which he founded in 1990. He graduated from the Royal College of Art and has since designed for NEC, Canon and Sony, amongst others, as well as creating eyewear for Seiko, lights for Daiko and toys for Hasbro. Davey was one of the first British designers to establish successful business links with Japanese manufacturers, and TKO's Japanese client base continues to grow. TKO also works for major companies in the USA and Europe. Davey and his team have won many design prizes including the 1996 BBC Design Award for Best Product, the BBC Designer of the Year, and Best of Category in the consumer products section of ID''s Annual Design Review for the Freeplay clockwork radio. – 182

Rolf Degel studied design at the Hochschule für Gestaltung, Offenbach, Germany. He worked for various design companies on a freelance basis before setting up his own environmental design office in 1994. – 204

Chanan de-Lange was born in 1955 and graduated from the Department of Industrial Design at the Bezalel Academy of Art and Design in Jerusalem. In 1987 he opened his own studio and started to teach at the Bezalel Academy where he was head of the Department of Industrial Design from 1992–95. He has taken part in many group exhibitions in Israel and Japan and has held one-man shows at the Amy Steinitz Gallery in Tel Aviv and at the Tel Aviv Museum of Art. – 135

Michele de Lucchi was born in Ferrara, Italy, in 1951 and graduated from Florence University in 1975. During his student years he founded the Gruppo Cavat, a group concerned with avant-garde and conceptual architecture. He worked and designed for Alchimia until the establishment of Memphis in 1981. He was responsible for the design of the Memphis exhibitions, and his most important works included a series of new

Biographies

household appliances and the prefabricated holiday houses which were shown at the Triennale in 1979 and 1983. Today he produces art-orientated handmade products, industrial consumer items and furniture in wood, metal, stone and other materials. He continues to be interested in avant-garde design: in 1986 he founded and promoted Solid, a group of young designers developing new design concepts, and in 1990, Produzione Privata, a production company for experimental objects. His architectural activities range from shop design to large-scale office buildings and private apartment blocks. De Lucchi has taught at design schools and universities such as the Domus Academy, Milan, and the University of Detroit. For the last two years he has held seminars on design management for the MBA course at the Università Commerciale Luigi Bocconi in Milan. – 75, 99, 136, 180

Marian de Rond was born in Hoeven in The Netherlands. In 1989 she received a Dutch State Stipendium which allowed her to study menswear design. She attended the Academy of Arts 'Den Bosch' from 1981 to 1986 and in 1983 undertook a course in woven fabrics. She has also studied fashion design. De Rond has worked for various fashion houses in Paris, Holland, The Netherlands and Milan, and since 1992 has worked on a freelance basis designing and making patterns and prototypes, and researching materials and details for collections of skiwear. – 206–7

Christian Deuber is part of the N2 group in Lucerne, Switzerland. While training as an electrical engineer, he gained experience in lighting design and set up his own studio, Pharus Lighting Design, in 1995. – 101

Jos Devriendt is a teacher at the Academy of Arts in Bruges, Belgium. He has exhibited his ceramic pieces in The Netherlands and at the Gallery Si Jun in Tokyo. – 108

Javier Diez Blanco and Jose Luis Diez Blanco were born in Madrid in 1966 and 1968, respectively. Javier studied industrial design at the Experimental Design School, Madrid; Jose Luis studied interior design at the Interior Design School, Madrid. From 1994 to 1997 they collaborated with B & R Arquitectos Asociados and Proun on architecture, interiors and furniture design. In 1996 they designed the carpet Vertigo for Bd Ediciones de Diseño. Diez and Diez have won awards for their work in Spain, most recently with the Miradas carpet and Aurea light. – 145

David D'Imperio was born in Pennsylvania in 1960. He graduated from Kutztown University with a degree in graphic design in 1982. In 1986 he received a US invention patent for his integrated marine aquarium. In 1990 he opened a studio in Miami producing exhibit designs for such clients as Bergdorf Goodman, Donna Karan, Royal Viking Cruises and Polygram Records. Since then he has established a reputation as a designer of hand-crafted lighting and has been represented in shows of American craft at the Smithsonian Institution, Washington, and the Philadelphia Museum of Art. – 102

Donato D'Urbino and Paolo Lomazzi were born in Milan in 1935 and 1936, respectively. In the 1960s they created a series of inflatable designs, which culminated in their inflatable chair Blow, in 1967. They have designed for Acerbis, Artemide, Driade, Disform and others, and have extended their work to include architecture, product and lighting design. Examples of their work can be found in the permanent collections of the Museum of Modern Art, New York; the Victoria and Albert Museum and Design Museum in London; the Centre Georges Pompidou in Paris; the Kunstgewerbe Museum in Zurich; the Staatliches Museum für Angewandte Kunst in Munich; and the Israel Museum in Jerusalem. – 200

Mark Dziersk is vice president of Herbst LaZar Bell Inc. He received a BFA in Industrial Design from the University of Michigan and is a member of the Industrial Designers Society of America. In addition to his work as a senior consultant and design manager for several leading design firms, he has worked as a corporate designer for the GenRad Corporation. Dziersk has held positions as adjunct professor at the Rhode Island School of Design in Providence and the New England School of Art and Design in Boston. He has received national acclaim for his designs, including the IDSA Industrial Design Excellence Award, Instrumentation. He holds 26 product design and engineering patents in the USA. – 180

Erwin Egli studied lighting design at the Zurich College of Decorative Arts from 1963–67. He worked for Alumag-Belmag, Louis Poulson and Co. and Verner Panton Binningen before setting up his own lighting, planning and lamp design company in 1988. He was awarded the Good Industrial Design Award in 1996 in Hanover for the Trapez light for Ribag Licht. – 96, 97

Egon Eiermann (1904–1970) was born in Neuendorf, Germany. He studied architecture at the Technische Hochschule in Charlottenburg under Hans Poelzig from 1923–27. He worked as an architect in the office of Rudolf Karstadt in Hamburg and for the Berlin electricity works before going into private practice in 1930. In 1946 he moved to Karlsruhe where he lived and worked until his death. From 1947–70 he was Dean of the Faculty of Architecture at Karlsruhe University. His work received much acclaim: he was awarded the Berlin Art Prize (1962); the Nordrhein-Westfalen State Prize (1965); the Cross of Merit of the German Federal Republic (1968); and the Grand Prize of the Bund Deutscher Architekten (1968). He built the German Pavilion at the Brussels World Fair in 1958 and completed numerous public commissions including the Kaiser-Wilhelm Memorial Church in Berlin (1957–63), the Members Building, Bundestag, Bonn (1965–69) and the German Embassy in Washington (1958–64). He also built corporate headquarters for Olivetti and IBM. – 30–31

Thomas Eisl and Michael Englisch were born in 1947 and 1961, respectively. Eisl was born in Tyrol, Austria and moved to England in 1969. Englisch was born in Ailingen, Germany, and studied at the Fachhochschule für Gestaltung in Schwäbisch where he later worked as a CAD-system lecturer. For the past seven years he has worked for the office furniture manufacturer VOKO, and has been head of the design and marketing department since 1995. He has won the Frogjunior Award and the Bavarian State Prize and has received the IF Design Award Hanover twice. – 134

Michael Englisch see Thomas Eisl

André Feldmann and Arne Jacob Schultchen were born in 1964 and 1965, respectively, and have worked as a team since they met at the Hochschule für Bildende Künste, Hamburg from which they graduated in industrial design in 1992/93. In 1994 they established their own studio in Hamburg. Their work ranges from product design, furniture, lighting and interior design to graphics, packaging, exhibition design and experimental works. – 211

Marco Ferreri was born in Imperia, Italy, in 1958 and graduated in architecture from Milan Polytechnic in 1981. He has worked for Robots (as art director), Danese, Fontana Arte, Luxo, Nemo, Osram, Agape, BPA, Adele C and Giorgetti. His Is stool is in the permanent collection of the Museum of Modern Art, New York. – 199

Thomas Ferwagner served an apprenticeship as a cabinet maker before studying interior and furniture design at the Kunstakademie in Stuttgart. In 1989 he founded his own studio, Officium, with Ina Ferwagner and has since been involved with industrial and furniture design, fair and exhibition design, television-set design, and architecture for zoos. He has exhibited throughout Germany and in Canada and has received awards for his work, most recently the Stahlinnovationspreis, Düsseldorf, in 1997. – 29

David Field has a degree in industrial design and a Masters degree in furniture design from the Royal College of Art where he has taught since 1979. He works as an exhibition organizer and consultant to national trade, design and craft bodies, as well as designing and manufacturing contract and domestic furniture. He is the originator and organizer of Spectrum, the only UK exhibition of design-led contract products companies, held annually at the Royal College of Art. In 1995 Field was made an MBE for his services to the arts. – 66–7

Sir Norman Foster was born in Manchester, England, in 1935 and studied architecture and city planning at the University of Manchester and

at Yale University. He established Team 4 in 1963 – with his late wife, Wendy, and Su and Richard Rogers – and founded Foster Associates in 1967. Today he is internationally famous for his high-tech designs, many of which have resulted directly from competitions, such as the Hong Kong and Shanghai Bank (1979–85), and Stansted Airport (1981–89). Recent projects include the Sackler Galleries at the Royal Academy of Arts, London which was named the RIBA building of the year in 1993; the Centre d'Art Cultural, Nîmes; the Reichstag remodelling, Berlin; new headquarters for Commerzbank in Frankfurt; and a new airport at Chek Lap Kok for Hong Kong, which at 1,248 hectares is one of the largest projects in the world. Masterplans include the King's Cross development, London. Foster received a knighthood in the Queen's Birthday Honours in 1991, and his work has won over 60 awards and citations. Although primarily concerned with large-scale architectural projects, Foster is also active in furniture and product design. – 201

Henrik Frederiksen was born in Aalborg, Denmark, in 1967. He attended the Danish Design School in Copenhagen and has had his own design practice since his graduation in 1995. – 36

Michal Fronek and Jan Nemecek were born in 1966 and 1963, respectively. Both studied at the Academy of Applied Arts in Prague under Borek Sipek. They began their first collaboration as the design group Olgoj Chorchoj shortly after attending a summer workshop at the Vitra Design Museum, and since then they have completed numerous interior design projects in Prague. Artel II was founded in 1993 and exhibited at the Milan Furniture Fair; the International Conference of Arts and Crafts, London; the International Design Exhibition, Turin; and the Gallery Genia Loci, Prague. Fronek and Nemecek have taught alongside Sipek at the Academy of Applied Arts in Prague and were responsible for designing the interior fittings in Vaclav Havel's Prague house. Recent commissions include the design of a fire staircase at the Academy of Fine Arts; the design of a jeans shop and sport shop in Bratislava; and the reconstruction and interior design of a penthouse for Elle magazine (all 1996). In 1997 they received an Honourable Award, Grand Prix of the Czech Association of Architects. – 71, 72, 106–7, 114, 137

Tatsuro Funahashi was born in Nagoya, Japan, in 1940. He is a product designer for and director of the Chubu Design Research Center Co., and is executive director for the Aichi Designers Union. He lectures at the Nagoya University of Arts, and specializes in the use of wood. – 89, 136

Helmut Galler was born in Salzburg, Austria, and studied architecture at the Technical University of Vienna. He works in Vienna and Vorarlberg. – 68

Gill Gane has been the director of the Neudorf Ceramic Company since 1979, creating limited production studio ceramics for clients worldwide. – 110

Jorge Garcia Garay was born in Buenos Aires and has worked in Barcelona since 1979 as the director of Garcia Garay Design. He is involved almost exclusively with lighting design, and his work can be seen in permanent collections in Europe and the United States. – 100

Adrien Gardere trained as a cabinet maker at the Ecole Supérieure des Arts Appliqués Boulle, Paris, before studying furniture design at the Ecole Nationale Supérieure des Arts Décoratifs. He has designed furniture for the new Bibliothèque Nationale in Paris and has exhibited his one-off marquetry pieces throughout France. – 96

Juan Gaspar was born in Barcelona in 1966 and studied industrial design in Barcelona. He began working as a designer with Lluis Porgueras, creating minimalist light fittings. In 1991 he founded his own practice, Tabula Rasa, and in 1995 began working for Marset Iluminacion. – 79

Jakob Gebert was born in Freiburg, Germany. He worked as a social worker and in community service until 1989 when he undertook practical training in architecture until 1994. At the same time he studied interior, product and building design at the Basle Academy of Design. In 1994 he founded his own studio in Weil am Rhein and has collaborated with Nils Holger Moorman since 1995, developing the Spanoto table. – 73

Daniel Gilgen was born in 1964. He received a degree from the Hochschule für Gestaltung, Offenbach. From 1990–91 he was an intern with Hollington Associates in London, and later worked for Vent Design in the USA before founding Studio Gilgengolla with M. Edler-Golla in Offenbach. In 1994 he created Faktor Produktgestaltung in Frankfurt am Main, specializing in the design of computer hardware and ecologically responsible didactic products. He has received many awards within Germany, most recently the Designauswahl Industrie Forum in Hanover. – 204

Nuala Goodman was born in Dublin, Ireland, in 1962. She studied at the National College of Art and Design, receiving a diploma in 1984. She travelled to Milan with a scholarship from the Italian Cultural Institute and worked for a short period with Sottsass Associati. Today she lives and works in Milan where she has painted collections of clothing for the principal boutiques in Italy, designed textile collections for avant-garde printing companies and designed products for Alessi and Swatch. She occasionally collaborates with Marianna Kennedy and James Howett in London on small furniture and product commissions for private clients. In 1995 she produced a series of sculptural paintings, part of which formed the subject of an exhibition which travelled to Dublin and Milan. – 168

Tobias Grau was born in Hamburg in 1957. He studied design in New York at the Parsons School of Design, then worked in the design and development office of Knoll International in Pennsylvania. He founded Tobias Grau KG with his wife, Franziska Grau, in Hamburg in 1984, producing light designs for his own collection. Graudesign was set up four years later and under this name he redesigns hotels and showrooms and was responsible for the corporate identity of forty branches of the jeans shop Werdin. He also produces series of furniture and product designs for various clients. He received an ID magazine award, New York, in 1993. – 85

Konstantin Grcic was born in 1965 in Germany. He trained as a cabinet maker and continued his education at the John Makepeace School for Craftsmen and the Royal College of Art, London. He is currently working as a freelance furniture designer in London and Munich for companies including ClassiCon, Cappellini, Authentics, SCP, Montina and Plaza Design, Tokyo. Interior design projects include a private house in Bad Homburg and a presentation for Authentics at the Ambiente Fair in 1995. – 49, 62

Kurt Greter was born in 1945 in Cham, Switzerland. He studied architecture and interior design in Zug and Lucerne and has since collaborated with Colboc in Paris and Renten Howard Wood Architects in London. He has had his own practice in Zurich since 1970, specializing in interior and furniture design. – 49

Alfredo Häberli was born in Buenos Aires in 1964 and studied industrial design at the Hochschule für Gestaltung in Zurich. He graduated in 1991 and in the same year started his collaboration with Christophe Marchand with a research grant from IKEA. They founded their own studio in 1993, and have since held over a hundred exhibitions. Clients include Alias, Driade, Luceplan, Authentics and Thonet. – 113, 200

Leif Hagerup founded his workshop in 1983, specializing in the production of rattan furniture which he studied in Indonesia. He began his training as an industrial designer in 1986 and was employed by Knud Holscher Design from 1990–93. He opened his own drawing office in 1993, designing the Chip chair and starting to develop the Dolphin bicycle trailer which has earned him many prizes including the Danish Design Award in 1997. He currently designs furniture, bicycle stands, advertising posters and other objects. – 208

Annaleena Hakatie was educated at the University of Art and Design in Helsinki, and undertook special studies at the Orrefors Glass School and the Pilchuck Glass School. She has taken part in group exhibitions in Scandinavia and at the University of Sunderland in England, and has held one-man shows in Helsinki and Sweden. She has been a part-time lecturer at the University of Art and Design in Helsinki and today works for littala Glass. – 115

Noa Hanyu was born in Kanagawa, Japan, in 1965. He graduated from the Department of Product Design at the Tama Art University, Tokyo. He worked at GK Planning and Design, Tokyo, from 1989–90. Awards for his work include the Grand Prix of the Japan Craft Expo and the Grand Prix of the Takaoka Craft Competition, both 1996. – 69, 112

Marc Harrison is an Australian designer who started his career as a builder and manufacturer of boats. He studied at Queensland College of Art, then established his own design and manufacturing business. He is currently mass-producing four designs and continuing to produce one-off pieces of furniture. – 131

Makio Hasuike was born in Tokyo in 1938 and graduated from the University of Arts in Tokyo in 1962. Since then he has worked as a designer in Milan, creating his own company, Fizzonasco, in 1983, specializing in fashion bags and articles for the office under the trademark MHWay. He has received many awards for his work including a gold medal for exposition preparation and artwork at the Milan Triennale in 1973 and the Compasso d'Oro in 1979. His brush container Cucciolo can be found in the permanent collection of the Museum of Modern Art, New York. – 201

Lars Hellsten studied sculpture and ceramics at the College of Art, Craft and Design in Stockholm, and has worked for Orrefors since 1972. His work can be found in many of the major design collections including the Stedelijk Museum, Amsterdam; the Kunstmuseum, Düsseldorf; the National Museum of Art, Kyoto, Japan; and the Victoria and Albert Museum, London. Since 1973 he has taken part in numerous exhibitions, notably 'Lars Hellsten – Retrospective Works' at the Galleri Orrefors (1992) and 'Lars Hellsten, Orrefors and Oran Warff, Kosta' at the Vaxjo Glass Museum (1994). – 128

Matthew Hilton was born in Hastings, England, in 1957. He studied furniture design at Kingston Polytechnic, Surrey, until 1979, then worked for several years as an industrial designer in London. He started his own design work in 1984, designing for SCP, Disform, XO, Idee, Alterego and Driade. He exhibits his work regularly at the Milan and Cologne Furniture Fairs. – 43

Herbert Hirche was born in Görlitz, Germany, in 1910. He served an apprenticeship as a carpenter, then from 1930–33 studied at the Bauhaus under Mies van der Rohe and Lilly Reich. He has been Professor of Architecture at the Hochschule für Angewandte Kunst in Berlin, and from 1952 taught interior architecture and furniture design in Stuttgart. Hirche was president of the German Society of Industrial Desigers (UDID) from 1960–70 and vice-chancellor of the Kunstakademie in Stuttgart from 1968–71. – 32–3

Geoff Hollington was born in Essex, England, and studied at Central Saint Martin's College and the Royal College of Art in London. He founded Hollington in 1980 and started his long-term collaboration with Herman Miller in the United States designing award-winning office furniture products. He has a large portfolio of clients including Parker Pen, and designs a range of objects from chairs to digital telephones. – 134, 199

Mike Holroyd was educated at St. Catherine's College, Cambridge, where he received a Masters degree in engineering. He worked for Rolls-Royce and PA Consulting Group before joining Norton Healthcare in 1993 where he is Director of Device Engineering and Director of Inhalation Technology. His Easi-Breathe Breath-Operated Inhaler received the Prince of Wales Award for Innovation in 1997. – 209

Knud Holscher was born in 1930. He studied at the School of Architecture, Royal Academy of Fine Arts, Copenhagen, and has since been responsible for numerous large-scale works in Norway, as well as smaller projects in France, Germany, Switzerland, Austria, Bahrain and the UK. Today he is a partner of Krohn and Hartvig Rasmussen Architects and Planners with whom he has worked since 1968. From 1968 to 1988 he was professor at the School of Architecture, Royal Academy of Fine Arts, and in 1979 was made a member of the Danish Design Council. In 1990 he became design consultant for Erco Leuchten, Germany, and was awarded a prize from the Industrie Forum Design, Hanover for a range of lamps designed for that company in 1993. – 204, 205

Niels Hvass was born in 1958. He studied furniture and instrument design at the Skolen for Brugskunst and metalwork at the Århus Kunstakademi before setting up his own design studio. He received the Kulturministeriets Design Award in 1995 and since 1992 has taught at Danmarks Designskole. – 37

James Irvine was born in London in 1958 and graduated from the Royal Academy of Art in 1984. He then moved to Italy and worked as a consultant designer for Olivetti with Ettore Sottsass and Michele de Lucchi. He participated in '12 New Memphis 86' and became a member of the group Solid. In 1987 Olivetti arranged a cultural exchange for Irvine with Toshiba in Tokyo, where he carried out research in industrial design. On his return to Milan he designed industrial products for Olivetti with Michele de Lucchi and became responsible for a new range of mini-computers and work-stations. In 1988 he set up his own studio in Milan, designing interiors, furniture and industrial products and collaborating with companies including Alessi, Cappellini and Fantini. In 1990 Irvine was a visiting lecturer at the Domus Academy, Milan. He held his first personal exhibition at the Royal College of Art, London, in 1993. – 16–17

Yoshifumi Ishikawa was born in Tokyo in 1961. He graduated from the Tamagawa University in 1994 and joined Canon Inc. His designs include the EX1-Hi camcorder and the Prima Super 28v camera. – 176

Setsu Ito was born in Yamaguchi, Japan, in 1964. He obtained a Masters degree in product design from the University of Tsukuba and has since published studies on product semantics and design valuations for the Japanese Society for the Science of Design. He has undertaken design research projects for the TDK Corporation, NEC Electric Co. and Nissan Motor Co., and in 1989 worked for Studio Alchimia in Milan. Since 1989 he has collaborated with Angelo Mangiarotti and has become a consultant designer for the TDK Corporation, with Bruno Gregori. – 47

Dorte Østergaard Jakobsen was born in Denmark in 1957 and graduated from the College of Arts and Crafts, Copenhagen, in 1984. He became a member of the textile group Emballage for two years before spending a year in Italy teaching at Milan Polytechnic. Today he is a partner in the textile and furniture group Alive Design, along with the industrial designer Jakob Berg. Jakobsen frequently exhibits his work in Denmark and has also shown in Sweden, Germany and Italy. – 167

Feliksas Jakubauskas was born in Lithuania in 1949. From 1974–76 he attended the Lithuanian Academy of Arts in Vilnius and from 1976–80 trained in the Tapestry Department of the Academy of Applied Arts in Budapest, Hungary. He has held solo exhibitions in Lithuania and Norway, and has taken part in exhibitions throughout the world, including the international textile exhibition 'Visions-Convergence' in Minneapolis, USA, in 1994 and 'Graz ITS' in Graz, Austria. His work can be seen in museum collections in Vilnius. – 148–51

Steve Jones studied industrial design at Newcastle Polytechnic, England, and worked as a consultant for various furniture companies before joining DPG in 1994. – 181

Johannes Kiessler was born in Munich in 1969. Since graduating from the Art Center College of Design in Switzerland he has worked for Studio De Lucchi as design consultant and personal assistant to Michele de Lucchi. His clients include Olivetti, Siemens, Mandarina Duck, Samsung and BMW, and for the Produzione Privata range he has designed the table lamp, Elio. In 1997 he and Michele de Lucchi were awarded the 'Premio SMAU' for a specialized banking printer (PR2) for Olivetti. Kiessler's design team also won the 'Best of Category' award of the ID Annual Design Review for a research project on future electronics in the domestic environment conducted for Olivetti, Philips and Cappellini. – 180

Hiroyuki Kimura was born in Ibaraki, Japan, in 1960. He graduated from the Nihon College of Art in 1982 and joined Canon where he has designed cameras and lenses. – 176

Valerie Kiock was born in Germany in 1971. She has just completed a three-year course in graphic design at the School of Design in Zurich and is part of the N2 group in Lucerne. – 40

Poul Kjaerholm (1929–1980) was a leading Danish designer of modern furniture using mainly steel, wood, marble, cane and leather. He studied design, and later lectured, at the Copenhagen School of Arts and Crafts. His designs have been manufactured by Fritz Hansen, E. Kold Christiensen and Ejnar Pedersen's P.P. Furniture. – 34

Ruud-Jan Kokke was born in Velp, The Netherlands, in 1956 and was educated at the Academy of Fine Arts in Arnhem. He started his own practice in 1986 designing numerous interiors and one-off furniture pieces. His work can be seen in the Museum of Modern Art, New York; the Cooper-Hewitt Museum, New York; the Stedelijk Museum, Amsterdam; and the Museum für Angewandte Kunst in Cologne, Germany. – 70

Sirkka Könönen studied at the Institute of Industrial Arts in Helsinki, Finland. She has exhibited her textile and knitwear widely throughout the Scandinavian countries and has also held solo shows in Japan, France and Switzerland. She has designed stage decorations and costumes for Finnish television and has managed her own company since 1991. – 165, 168

Hanna Korvela was born in 1968 in Finland and studied at the Kuopio Academy of Crafts and Design where she received a degree in textile design in 1994. She is currently working in home textiles and has also created textiles for a Lutheran church and wall sculptures for public spaces. – 154

Anne Kosonen is a Finnish interior designer who has run her own design studio since 1991. She studied at the University of Industrial Design in Helsinki and today specializes in home furnishings. – 97

Peter Kunz was born in Switzerland in 1964. After studying architecture he founded his own studio in 1990. He designs mainly industrial plants and domestic houses, collaborating with the manufacturing companies Radius in Germany and Spichtig in Switzerland. – 185

Erik-Jan Kwakkel was educated at the Art Academy of Arnhem, The Netherlands, in the Department of Three-dimensional Design. He designs mainly tableware products in porcelain and ceramics. He was the winner of the Ceramic Design Award in 1992 and has held numerous exhibitions in The Netherlands and abroad. Several of his products are in the design collections of museums including the Museum Boymans-Van Beuningen in Rotterdam. – 117, 188, 190–1

Erika Lagerbielke studied industrial design and has been employed by Orrefors since 1982. She has held joint and one-woman shows throughout Scandinavia as well as at the Orrefors Crystal Galleries in New York and Los Angeles. – 115

Janja Lap works in Slovenia as a university lecturer and freelance designer. She regularly takes part in exhibitions, and her Laser Stimulator canbe seen in the permanent collection of Die Neue Sammlung in Munich. Her work has been published in Domus magazine and in many Slovenian publications and catalogues. – 129

Jack Lenor Larsen was born in 1927 in Seattle, USA. He studied furniture design but his real interest lay in fabric design and he founded his international fabric company in 1953. In 1959 he was responsible for producing the first printed velvets and in 1961 the first stretch upholsteries. From 1957–59 he was the consultant to the State Department for a grass-weaving project in Taiwan and Vietnam, after which he became co-director of the Fabric Design Department at the Philadelphia College of Art in Pennsylvania. He has been an artist in residence at the Royal College of Art, London, and was the curator of 'Wall Hangings' at the Museum of Modern Art, New York. From 1981–89 Larsen was president of the American Craft Council, becoming President Emeritus in 1990. In 1992 he founded the LongHouse Foundation in East Hampton, New York. He has received numerous awards for his work, most recently the Brooklyn Museum Design Award for Lifetime Achievement (1993). – 155

Sandra Laube see Biagio Cisotti

Jos Laugs was born in 1958 in Niewstadt, The Netherlands. He trained at the Academy of Fine Arts in Maastricht, and since 1992 has taught product design and product presentation at the College of Higher Education in Sittard. He is a self-employed designer of furniture and interiors for corporate and private clients, and founded the firm Furnitura to market his cabinets, tables and chairs. – 60

Stefan Lippert studied industrial design at the Kunstakademie in Stuttgart under Richard Sapper. Since 1994 he has had his own design firm and works for clients in the sports and medical fields including Uvex, Addidas and Pro Activ. – 208

Josep Lluscà was born in Barcelona in 1948. He studied industrial design at the Escola Eina, where he is now professor, and at the Ecole des Arts et Métiers, Montreal. He was vice-president of ADI-FAD (Industrial Designers' Association) from 1985–87, and was one of the founding members of the ADP (Association of Professional Designers). He is also a member of the Design Council of the Catalonian government. He has been the recipient of several major awards, including the 1990 National Design Award and two prizes from the Design Award in Furniture presented by ID magazine, New York (1993), as well as an Honorable Mention in Furniture in 1995. He also received the AEPD Award of Design in 1995 from the Spanish Association of Professionals for a series of emergency lights designed for Daisalux. He frequently attends international exhibitions and conferences, most recently 'Catalonia 90's' in New York and 'International Design' at the Design Museum, London. – 45, 94

Glen Oliver Loew was born in Leverkusen, Germany, in 1959. He studied at the University of Wuppertal, receiving a degree in industrial design in 1985. He then moved to Milan and studied for a Masters degree at the Domus Academy. He has collaborated with Antonio Citterio since 1987, becoming a partner in his studio in 1990. Together they have worked for such companies as Vitra, Kartell, Flos, Olivetti and Bieffe. Loew received a Compasso d'Oro in 1995 for his Mobil system for Kartell. He has also worked in corporate design, creating the retail system for the fashion-company Cecil (1991) and new corporate images for Commerzbank (1996) and Smart Centers (1997). – 44

Paolo Lomazzi see Donato D'Urbino

Christianna Los studied Fine Art at the Byam Shaw School of Drawing and Painting, London. She designed and sold knitwear in Scotland before undertaking a postgraduate course in textiles at Goldsmiths' College, specializing in tapestry weaving. Since 1988 she has worked on commissions

Biographies

for private clients in the South of France and Monaco. She is an active member of the national exhibiting group, New Fibre Art, and of the Society of Designer-Craftsmen. She received an award for her work from the Hellenic Foundation in 1993 and from the Theo Moorman Charitable Trust in 1996 for the development of her technique. – 152

Daniele Lo Scalzo Moscheri was born in 1962 and graduated from the Faculty of Architecture at Milan University in 1987. The following year he received a Masters degree in advanced technology application on industrial design manufacture from Tampa University in Florida. He was an associate in the studio of Piero Lissoni before setting up his own practice with Maurizio Maselli. Since the beginning of 1997 he has been art director of Piacenza Cashmere sales outlets. – 51

Ross Lovegrove was born in 1958 in Wales. He graduated from Manchester Polytechnic in 1980 with a Bachelor of Arts degree in industrial design, later receiving an Mdes from the Royal College of Art, London. He has worked for various design consultancies including Allied International Designers, London, and Frogdesign in Germany. In 1984 he moved to Paris to work for Knoll International and became a member of the Atelier de Nîmes, a group of five designers which included Gérard Barrau, Jean Nouvel, Martine Bedin and Philippe Starck. In 1986 he co-founded Lovegrove and Brown Design Studio which was later replaced by Lovegrove Studio X. Clients include Louis Vuitton, Luceplan, Tag Heuer, Philips, Sony and Apple Computers. His work can be seen in major design collections throughout Europe and in the Museum of Modern Art, New York. Lovegrove is a visiting lecturer at the Royal College of Art. – 38

Roberto Lucci and Paolo Orlandini were born in 1942 and 1941, respectively. Lucci was born in Milan and studied design at the Institute of Design in Chicago and at the Corso Superiore di Disegno Industriale in Venice. Orlandini was born in Grosseto and graduated in architecture from Milan Polytechnic. They have both worked for Marco Zanuso Sr and Richard Sapper. They started their partnership in 1968 and since then have designed over 200 products ranging from furniture for companies such as Knoll, Biesse and Artemide, to boats for Conaver and Pirelli, and children's products for Peg Perego Pines. Since starting their practice they have received many design awards, from the Compasso d'Oro (1979, '81, '84, '89 and '91) to, most recently, the Industrial Design Distinction Award, New York (1996). – 57

David Lynch was born in Missoula, Montana, in 1946. He was educated at the Boston Museum School and the Pennsylvania Academy of Fine Arts in Philadelphia. Today he is one of America's leading film directors, famous for such films as Eraserhead, The Elephant Man, Dune, Blue Velvet, Wild at Heart, Lumiere and Company and The Lost Highway. He also worked on the popular television series Twin Peaks from 1989–90. There have been many major retrospectives of his work at venues such as the American Museum of the Moving Image, New York; the British Film Institute, London, and Pennsylvania Academy of the Fine Arts. He has also held solo exhibitions worldwide. – 22–3

Vico Magistretti was born in Milan in 1920 and graduated with a degree in architecture from Milan Polytechnic in 1945. Since 1967 he has been a member of the Academy of San Luca in Rome, as well as teaching at the Domus Academy in Milan. He is also an honorary member of the Royal College of Art in London, where he is a visiting professor. He has been the recipient of numerous major awards including the Gold Medal at the Milan Triennale in 1951, the Compasso d'Oro in 1967 and 1979 and the Gold Medal of the Society of International Artists and Designers in 1986. Magistretti's buildings are primarily found in Italy, but his furniture, lamps and other designs are known internationally. He has worked for companies including Alias, Artemide, Cassina, de Padova, Fiat, Knoll International and Rosenthal. – 18–19, 28

Hans Maier-Aichen was born in Stuttgart, Germany, in 1940. He studied interior design at the Academy of Applied Arts in Wuppertal and Fine Art at the State University of Fine Arts, Munich. He has taught at the Art Institute of Chicago, the Academy of Fine Arts, Münster, and the National Academy of Fine Arts, Karlsruhe. He joined Artipresent GmbH in 1974 as managing director and created the Authentics trademark in 1980. From 1978–85 Maier-Aichen was the consultant on cultural affairs for the European Community, Brussels. – 196

Enzo Mari was born in Novara, Italy, in 1932 and studied at the Accademia di Belle Arti in Milan. In 1963 he co-ordinated the Italian group Nuove Tendenze and in 1965 was responsible for the exhibition of optical, kinetic and programmed art at the Biennale in Zagreb. He has also taken part in several Biennali in Venice and in the Milan Triennale. In 1972 he participated in 'Italy: The New Domestic Landscape' at the Museum the Compasso d'Oro on three occasions and was President of the Association for Industrial Design from 1976–79. His work can be found in the collections of various contemporary art museums including the Stedelijk Museum, Amsterdam; the Musée des Arts Décoratifs, Paris; and the Kunstmuseum, Düsseldorf. – 48, 119–22, 123, 137, 138, 193, 199

Jonathan Marshall received a Bachelor of Arts degree from the Product Design Department of Ravensbourne College of Design and Communication, Kent, England, in 1992. He worked for two years as a designer for Absolute Design Consultants in London, and from 1994–96 studied for a Masters degree in industrial design at the Royal College of Art. He is currently working with Ross Lovegrove at Studio X. – 202

Gussena Martin is a student with YA/YA Design, New Orleans, and is also studying commercial design at the L.E. Rabouin Career Magnet High School. Martin's work has been exhibited throughout the USA. – 161

Helena Mattila-Sorri studied law and was a financial analyst and credit manager until 1995 when she founded her own company Everyday Design. The company produces recyclable objects for everyday use made from paper and cardboard. – 97

Ingo Maurer was born in 1932 on the Island of Reichenau, Lake Constance, Germany, and trained in typography and graphic design. In 1960 he emigrated to the United States and worked as a freelance designer in New York and San Francisco before returning to Europe in 1963. He founded Design M in Munich in 1966, and since then his lighting designs have achieved world recognition. He has exhibited widely, in shows that include 'Ingo Maurer: Making Light' at the Museum Villa Stuck, Munich, and 'Licht Licht' at the Stedelijk Museum in Amsterdam, and his work is in the permanent collections of many museums including the Museum of Modern Art, New York. – 86, 103

Norberto Medardi studied architecture at Florence University. In 1988 he started a collaboration with David Palterer and in 1997 wrote a book on Palterer's work. Medardi's work has been published in design magazines such as Domus, Interni, Abitare, Architektur und Wohnen and DDN. – 127, 135

Kurt Meinecke was educated at the School of Fine Art, Washington University. In 1980 he founded the graphic design firm Group/Chicago, and his work has since been recognized by such organizations as the New York Art Director's Club, the American Institute of Graphic Arts and the American Center for Design. In 1996 he created the Meinecke Collection which has now expanded to include over 160 rug designs ranging from modern to ethnic and updated traditional designs. The collection received the ADEX Award for Area Rugs in 1996. – 158, 160, 163

Metz.Schlett.Kindler was founded by Guido Metz, Matthias Schlett and Michael Kindler, three product designers from the University of Darmstadt. The company is active in public design and tableware and aims to redefine traditional household objects working for manufacturers such as Authentics, Alessi and WMF. In 1992 and 1995 three projects won the exhibition at the Braun Design Prize, and in 1997 the Die Enyklopen cutlery was awarded the Sabattini Prize and the Knut ladle received a Design Plus award. – 140

Dagmar Mombach was born in 1958. She studied design at the University of Kassel, Germany, and since 1984 has collaborated with Ingo Maurer, from 1993 on the development of the MoMaNoughies light. – 103

Marcello Morandini was born in Mantua, Italy, in 1940. He studied at the Varese School of Arts before training as a graphic designer at the

Brera Academy in Milan. By 1968 he had opened studios in Genoa and Milan and, in collaboration with Umberto Eco, was involved in graphics and publishing. In 1980 he started his association with the architects Miraglia and Ong & Ong in Singapore, and has since designed façades for the Thomas plant in Speichersdorf, Germany; for the administrative building of the Rosenthal company in Selb, Bavaria; and for a 36-storey office building in Kuala Lumpur (not built). He has exhibited his work widely both nationally and internationally, taking part in Documenta, Kassel (1977, 1980), the Venice Biennale (1986) and the International Forum on Design in Ulm (1990), and holding individual shows in Hanover. In 1997 he became the director of the Ceramics Museum in Laveno, Lake Maggiore. – 146–7

Ulf Moritz graduated in 1960 from the Textilingenieurschule, Krefeld, Germany, and worked as a textile designer for Weverij de Ploeg before setting up his own design studio in 1970. His work includes collection co-ordination, corporate identity, art direction, exhibition stands and architectural projects. He has collaborated with Felice Rossi, Montis, Ruckstuhl, Interlübke and Interline Nova. The textile collection Ulf Moritz by Sahco Hesslein was established in 1986. His work is represented in the Stedelijk Museum, Amsterdam; the Cooper-Hewitt Museum, New York; and the Textielmuseum, Tilburg. Since 1971 he has been a professor at the Academy of Industrial Design in Eindhoven. – 153

Massimo Morozzi was born in Florence in 1941. Today he is an Associate of the CDM Group (Consulenti Design Milano). Clients include Alessi, Cassina, Driade, Fiam, Georgetti, Edra and Mazzei, and he has also developed designs for IRJ Corporate Image in Japan. Morozzi is art director of Edra and Mazzei. In 1990 he set up Morozzi and Partners with Silvia Centeleghe, Giovanni Lauda and Cristina Dossio Morozzi. He lectures in Amsterdam, San Paolo, Melbourne and at the Domus Academy and the Istituto Europeo di Disegno in Milan. – 24–5

Jeong Myungchul was born in Seoul, Korea, in 1964. He received a degree in architecture from Kookmin University, then went on to study in Rome and was awarded a diploma in interior design from the Istituto Europeo di Disegno. He has recently specialized in design management at Milan Polytechnic and since 1997 has collaborated with an architectural company in Seoul. His design Tea for Two was one of the top ten products at the International Chair Fair in Udine in 1996, and he was selected as one of the young designers of the year at the 1997 Milan Furniture Fair. – 46

Nicole Naas see Tom Bisig

Mikala Naur was born in Copenhagen in 1957. She trained as a goldsmith and has had her own studio since 1983. She has held many exhibitions in Denmark and has pieces in the permanent collections of the Museums of Modern Art in Copenhagen, Oslo and Trondheim. She designs both jewellery and decorative objects for the home. – 193

Jan Nemecek see Michal Fronek

Ninaber/Peters/Krouwel (N/P/K) Industrial Design was established in 1985 by Bruno Ninaber van Eyben, Wolfram Peters and Peter Krouwel with the aim of producing a wide variety of line-assembly and mass-produced products for the consumer and professional market. Ninaber graduated from Maastricht Art Academy in 1971, Peters and Krouwel from the Delft Technical University in 1978. Their work covers all stages from design through development to pre-production management. Their designs can be seen in the permanent collections of the Museum of Modern Art, New York; the Stedelijk Museum, Amsterdam; and the Design Museum, London, amongst others. In 1990 nine of their products received a Gute Industrieform recognition. – 210

Jean Nouvel was born in Fumel, Lot-et-Garonne, France, in 1945 and graduated in 1971. In 1976 he co-founded the Mars 1976 movement and rapidly became known as one of the leading French architects. He was made a Chevalier de l'Ordre du Mérite and a Chevalier des Arts et Lettres in 1983, and awarded the Grand Prix d'Architecture in 1987. In 1989 his Institut du Monde Arabe was voted the best French building of that year. He founded a partnership with Emmanuel Cattani in 1989 and together they worked on the CNRS Documentation Centre in Nancy (1989); the Poulain Factory in Blos (1991); the Hotel les Thermes in Dax (1992); and a shopping centre in Lille. Nouvel now has his own practice and has recently completed the Galerie Lafayette, Berlin. He produces furniture for manufacturers including Ligne Roset and Ecart. – 203

Kuno Nüssli was born in Switzerland in 1970. He served an apprenticeship as a carpenter from 1987–91, followed by an internship as a lighting designer. She then studied for a postgraduate degree in interior and product design at the School of Arts in Basle. From 1996–97 he was involved in the Recycling Stations project for the Department of Building in Basle. – 40

Saar Oosterhof was born in Utrecht, The Netherlands, in 1971. She studied fashion design at Utrecht School of Arts, followed by textile design at the Gerrit Rietveld Academy, Amsterdam, until 1996. Since 1997 she has been working as an independent designer. – 189

Paolo Orlandini see Roberto Lucci

Verner Panton was born in 1926 in Gamtofts, Denmark. He trained in architecture at the Copenhagen Royal Academy of Fine Arts and continued his studies in various European countries between 1953 and 1955. His innovative early designs included a series of architectural projects built between 1957 and 1960, notably the Cardboard House (1957) and Plastic House (1960). His work includes furniture, lighting, carpets, textiles and exhibitions. In 1960 he created his best-known design, the first one-piece cantilever plastic chair in a fibreglass shell, produced by Herman Miller from 1967. He has also designed numerous interior schemes including the Junior Casino, Germany (1973) and the Grüner and Jahr Publishing House, Hamburg (1974). He is a Fellow of the Royal Society of Arts, London, and until 1984 was a visiting professor in industrial design at the Hochschule für Gestaltung in Offenbach. – 35

UMS-Pastoe is a Dutch furniture design company, founded in 1913 as the Utrechtse Machinale Stoel- en Meubelfabriek. It originally catered for a traditional market as well as experimenting with modern, avant-garde designs. Since the Second World War, however, the company has concentrated entirely on contemporary furniture. – 50

Stefan Patte was born in 1963 in Coesfeld near Münster, Germany. He served an apprenticeship as a locksmith then, following a move to Munich, worked with a blacksmith, a stucco worker and as a technical specialist in a power plant before setting up his own studio in 1989. With a partner he founded Objektiv Design Ltd which later became Fürst and Patte Design, then Stefan Patte Design Ltd. His growing interest in alternative energy sources resulted in the formation of SolArt which exhibited for the first time in Cologne in 1996. – 199

Terri Pecora was born in 1958 in Idaho, in the USA, and grew up in California. She studied fashion illustration at the Art Centre College of Design in Pasadena, then moved to Milan in 1989, taking a course in product design at the Domus Academy. She established her own studio in 1991 and her clients include Authentics, Edra, Esprit, Silhouette, Swatch and Sech Ratan. Since 1996 she has concentrated almost exclusively on a new range of children's products which she designs and produces with her partner in Milan. – 206–7

Jiří Pelcl was born in 1950 in the Czech Republic. He studied architecture at the Academy of Applied Art in Prague and furniture design at the Royal College of Art in London. He is a founder member of the group Allka and since 1990 has run his own architectural/design studio, Atelier Pelcl. Major commissions include interiors for Vaclav Havel's study in Prague Castle (1990); St Laurence Church, Prague (1994); the Czech Embassy in Rome (1995); the Ministry of Foreign Affairs, Prague (1995); and Cernin's Palace in Prague (1995). He has exhibited in galleries in Prague, Brno, Vienna, Berlin, Munich, Amsterdam and Paris. –136, 141

Roberto Pezzetta was born in Treviso, Italy, in 1946. He began his career as a product designer in 1969 and has been head of Zanussi Elettrodomestici Industrial Design Centre since 1982. Although primarily associated with white goods, he has also been active in other fields of industrial design. With the Zanussi Industrial Design Centre he was awarded the Compasso d'Oro in 1981. His products were also selected at the Compasso d'Oro in 1987, 1989 and 1991, and he was presented an award from the Czech Republic in 1997. Pezzetta is currently director of design within the Electolux European Design Management. – 172–3

Stephen Philips studied at the Epsom College of Art and Design, Surrey, England, and at the Buckinghamshire College of Art and Design where he received a Bachelor of Arts degree in furniture design in 1992. He worked for SKK Lighting before opening his own studio, Stephen Philips Design UK, in 1994. He has taken part in design shows throughout Europe, and clients include The Conran Shop, Hampshire Architects, Harvey Nichols and Sears plc. – 88

Piero Polato currently works as a freelance designer for Nava Design in Milan and is known for his work in products, theatre, film and television. He is a consultant for the Ministry of Public Instruction and a researcher for UNESCO, as well as being Professor of Project Methodology at the Superior Institute of Design (ISIA), Urbino. Together with Bruno Munari he designed the 'To Play with Art' workshops in Brera, Milan and at the International Museum of Ceramics in Faenza. – 185

Gio Ponti (1891–1979) was born in Milan and completed his training as an architect at Milan Polytechnic in 1921. In 1923 he became artistic director of Richard Ginori. He founded Domus magazine in 1928. His work included residential buildings, public buildings, furniture, lighting, products, fabrics and tableware, and he also worked as a painter and stage-set designer. From 1936–61 he taught at Milan Polytechnic. He became Italy's best-known post-war architect. In the 1930s he built several buildings in Milan in the 'New Style', including the tower of the Corso Venezia, the Rai and Ferrania Palaces and the tower in Sempione Park. In 1956 he designed a multi-storey building to house the Italian firm of Pirelli. He also drew up the plans for well-known housing developments in Europe, the Middle East, Canada, USA and South America. – 63

Manolo Portaceli studied at the Higher Technical College of Architecture in Barcelona. He started his career teaching the history of architecture at the Technical College of Architecture in Valencia and continues to lecture widely and publish papers on design history and restoration. He has won many awards for his built work, including the Fibas Award for the restoration of the shipyards of Valencia (1994) and first prize in the competition for the restoration of the Neues Museum and the construction of the extension and connecting buildings for the exhibition of the archaelogical collections of the State Museums of Berlin. This scheme was also selected for the European Architecture Prize Mies van der Rohe in Berlin,1994. – 72

Julian Powell-Tuck graduated from the Royal College of Art, London, in 1976 with a Masters degree in Environmental Design. He set up his own practice shortly afterwards and has since earned an international reputation as an architect and designer. He frequently lectures at the Royal College of Art and Kingston University, Surrey. – 92

Paul Priestman is a founder member of Priestman Goode, a product and industrial design practice which was set up in London in 1986. Its designs cover a range of products including audio equipment, televisions, stationery, sporting goods, domestic appliances, luggage and furniture. It is also involved in the design of yacht interiors and motor cars. The practice has exhibited extensively throughout the world and has won international competitions in the Far East, Europe and the USA. – 210

Christopher Procter and Fernando Rihl both studied at the Architectural Association in London. They are well known for their experimental work in the use of live-edge acrylic in furniture design. Before starting their collaboration, Procter worked with the architects Rick Mather and Paolo Solari and the engineer Tim MacFarlane, and Rihl collaborated with the landscape architect Burle Marx. They worked with Zaha Hadid on panels for the Interbuild Blueprint Pavilion and in 1996 were commissioned to design acrylic partitions for a new shop in a Gio Ponti building in Hong Kong. The clothing chain Jigsaw have also commissioned panels for five shops in central London. Procter and Rihl's work can be seen in the design collection of the Museum of Modern Art in New York. – 51

Karim Rashid graduated in industrial design in 1982 from Carleton University in Ottawa, Canada. After graduate studies in Italy, he moved to Milan for a one-year scholarship in the studio of Rodolfo Bonetto. On his return to Canada he worked for seven years with KAN Industrial Designers in Toronto, designing projects ranging from high-tech products to furniture, and also designing the Babel and North clothing collections from 1985–90. Today he is a full-time Associate Professor of Industrial Design at the University of Arts in Philadelphia. He has also taught at the Pratt Institute, Rhode Island School of Design and Ontario College of Art. Since 1992 he has been principal designer for Karim Rashid Industrial Design in New York, designing products, lighting, tableware and furniture. He has won many awards including the Good Design Award/Permanent Collection (32 objects for Nambe Mills) in 1995 and ID 40 Leading Edge Designers from ID magazine in 1996. His work has been exhibited in museums internationally, including the Museum of Modern Art, New York; the Chicago Athenaeum; and the Design Museum, London. – 197, 200

Kristina Råström studied art history and Fine Art before undertaking a three-year course in furniture design at the Beckmans School of Design, Stockholm. In 1996 she received an Elle Interior Design Scholarship and has since specialized in carpet design and ceramics. In 1997 the Krickan carpet was exhibited at the Furniture Fairs in Cologne and Milan, and the Stockholm Art Fair. – 144

This Reber trained as a joiner and draughtsman before studying interior and product design at the School of Art in Basle. He has been working on architecture and furniture projects since 1996, and today is involved with the N2 group. – 62

Ann Richards trained initially as a biologist before studying woven textiles at the Surrey College of Art and Design, England, where she now teaches. She has exhibited her work in the UK and Japan, and in 1989 won first prize at the International Textile Design Contest in Tokyo. Her work is in a number of public collections including the Fashion Foundation, Tokyo, and the Crafts Council, London. – 154, 156

Fernando Rihl see Christopher Procter

Patrizio Roffi was born in Zurich in 1967. He studied graphic and interior design, then from 1989–91 worked as a freelance designer involved in graphics, illustration, interior design and the construction of trade fair stands. In 1991 he joined the product design development department of DNR Sportsystem Ltd, Switzerland. – 210

Vibeke Rohland studied art history at Copenhagen University, then worked at the Willumben Museum of Art. From 1982–86 she attended the Textile Department of the Copenhagen School of Decorative Arts. In 1987 she started work for Eliakim Création de Tissue in Paris where she was responsible for the handpainting of textiles for Parisian haute couture and produced a textile collection for the Japanese market. Since 1991 she has been working on a freelance basis for designers such as Esprit in Düsseldorf and New York and Agnès B in Paris. Exhibitions to date have included 'Textile Manifestation' at the Museum of Decorative Arts, Denmark (1988); 'Dansk Design Aktuelt' (1992); and numerous solo shows, most recently at the Borås Art Museum, Sweden (1996). In 1995 she was invited to design interiors and accessories for the Danish State Railways. – 156, 166

Julia Rosengarth studied interior design in Düsseldorf, specializing in furniture design. She has her own company in Hoffnungstal, near Cologne, and designs interiors for shops, bars, restaurants and trade fair stands. – 65

Alejandro Ruiz was born in 1958 in Bahía Blanca, Argentina. He studied industrial design in La Plata, graduating in 1984, and later received a Master's degree from the Domus Academy in Milan. He has collaborated with Studio Alchimia (1985–86) and Gregotti Associati International (1987–89) and founded his own studio in 1989. In 1994 he set up Lessdesign with Anna Lombardi to develop industrial products, working with clients such as Alessi, Authentics, Electrolux-Zanussi and Venini. One of his designs for Alessi is part of the permanent collection of the Museum of Modern Art in New York. – 194

Lino Sabattini was born in 1925 in Correggio, Italy. His metalwork first attracted international attention in 1956 when it was exhibited in Paris. Since then, he has continued to be closely associated with a simple, sculptural approach to metal and glassware, working for companies such as Rosenthal AG in Germany and Zani Metalwares in Italy. He has exhibited at the Milan Triennale on several occasions, and was awarded the Compasso d'Oro in 1979. His work is in the permanent collections of the British Museum and the Victoria and Albert Museum, London; and the Museum of Modern Art and Cooper-Hewitt Museum, New York. – 129

Masatoshi Sakaegi was born in 1944 in Chiba-ken, Japan. In 1983 he founded the Masatoshi Sakaegi Design Studio which specializes in ceramic and melamine tableware and ceramic sculpture. He has won many awards for his work, most recently at the 4th International Ceramics Competition in Mino, Japan, in 1995. In 1997 he was selected to be one of ten world-famous designers at the 50th 'Premio Faenza', the international exhibition of contemporary ceramics in Faenza, Italy. – 117

Timo Salli studied metalcraft and welding at the Keskipohjanaa Professional School, followed by a Bachelor of Arts degree in furniture design at Lahti Design Institute, Finland, and a Masters degree in draft and design at the University of Art and Design in Helsinki. He worked as a welder from 1982–89 and then for various design studios before founding his own practice in 1993. He has collaborated with Stefan Lindfors and Jussi Heikkila, and has carried out metal construction, design and manufacturing for Finnish firms such as Valvomo Ltd. – 41

Hector Santos was born in Manilla, The Philippines, in 1962. He studied mechanical engineering before graduating in industrial design from California State University, Long Beach, USA. He was a senior industrial designer at Ron Loosen Associates until 1992 when he established his own design firm, Pi Design. – 180

William Sawaya was born in Beirut in 1948 and graduated in 1973 from the National Academy of Arts. He worked in the USA and France before moving to Italy in 1978. With Paolo Moroni in 1984 he founded Sawaya and Moroni where he is artistic director and project manager. His work can be found in the permanent collections of the Israel Museum, Jerusalem; the Chicago Athenaeum; the Museum für Gestaltung, Basle; the Westerburg Museum, Bremen; the Kunsthal Museum, Rotterdam; and the Design Centre, Malmö. – 55

Winfried Scheuer was born in Calw, Germany, in 1952. He worked as a trainee in the styling department of Mercedes-Benz in Sindelfingen before studying at the Royal College of Art, London, from 1979–81. He has worked in London as a self-employed industrial designer since 1986 and has exhibited his work at Documenta Kassel and the Luci Exhibition, Memphis, Milan. He is a visiting lecturer at the Royal College of Art and at the Hochschule der Künste, Berlin. – 99, 193, 195, 197

Arne Jacob Schultchen see André Feldmann

Franz-Josef Schulte was born in Krefeld, Germany, in 1951. He studied interior architecture, receiving a diploma from the Fachhochschule in Düsseldorf in 1975. He worked with Peter Maly before opening his own design studio in Krefeld in 1978. Schulte Designforum was founded in 1991 and Schulte Design GmbH in 1993. Schulte has designed furniture for Rosenthal, De Sede, Walter Knoll and Egoform, and has been the recipient of many national awards including the Industrie Forum Design Hanover IF prize in 1993. – 50

Herbert H. Schultes was born in 1938. He studied engineering and design in Munich and from 1961–67 was employed by Siemens AG. He is the founder of the Industrial Design course at the Advanced Technical College in Munich. In 1967 he co-founded the Schlagheck Schultes Design Company, whilst still maintaining his links with Siemens, becoming head of design in 1985. Schultes is a board member of the Industrie Forum Design in Hanover and the Internationales Design Zentrum in Berlin. He is also chairman of the board and founder of the Design Zentrum in Munich. – 96

Tetsuya Sekine was born in Yokohama, Japan, in 1966. He graduated from the Nihon University College of Art in 1990 and joined Canon shortly afterwards, designing calculators, word processors and printers. – 180

Yasushi Shiotani was born in Tokyo in 1962 and graduated from the Tsukuba University in 1985. He joined Canon shortly afterwards, designingcases and accessories for cameras, interface for television conference systems and the IXUS camera. He studied at the Domus Academy in Milan for a year in 1993. – 177

Barbora Skorpilová was born in 1972. She studied construction and furniture design, then from 1991–97 attended the Applied Art Department of the University of Architecture and Design in Prague studying under Borek Sípek. At the same time she collaborated with the Czech design studio Olgoj Chorchoj. She has exhibited her work in the Czech Republic and in Milan and London. – 26, 126, 129

John Smith trained as a furniture designer in the UK before moving to Australia. He is head of furniture design at the University of Tasmania. –89

Penny Smith studied for a Bachelor of Arts degree in furniture design in the UK, graduating in 1969. In 1970 she emigrated to Tasmania, Australia. She established her first pottery shop three years later, followed by a further studio which specializes in semi-industrial processes. She is currently head of the ceramics studio and the Ceramic Research Unit at the School of Art, University of Tasmania. She is an artist-in-residence in Banff, Canada, and at the Arabia tableware factory in Helsinki, and has taken part in many solo and group exhibitions internationally. – 89

Peter Sonntag was born in Hamburg in 1960. After training and working as a cabinet maker he studied industrial design at the Hochschule für Bildende Künste. He has worked as a freelance designer since 1990, designing in collaboration with Tobias Grau since 1993. In 1993 he was made a partner of Hafenatelier, Hamburg. – 85

Ayala Sperling-Serfaty was born in Israel in 1962. Following early education and military service in Israel, she studied Fine Art at the Middlesex Polytechnic, England, and Art History and Philosophy at Tel Aviv University. She was awarded a scholarship from the Sharet Fund, Israel, in 1984 and presented with first prize in the Annual Furniture Design Competition in Israel in 1993. – 89

Ernesto Spicciolato see Santina Bonini

Philippe Starck was born in Paris in 1949. After a period of activity in New York, he returned to France where he has since built up an international reputation. He has been responsible for major interior design schemes, including François Mitterrand's apartment at the Elysée Palace; the Café Costes; and the Royalton and Paramount hotels in New York. He has also created domestic and public multi-purpose buildings such as the headquarters of Asahi Beer in Tokyo. As a product designer he works for companies throughout the world, collaborating with Alessi, Baleri, Baum, Disform, Driade, Flos, Kartell, Rapsel, Up & Up, Vitra and Vuitton. For the last three years he has been design director of domestic electronic products for the Thomson Group. His many awards include the Grand Prix National de la Création Industrielle. His work can be seen in the

Biographies

permanent collections of all the major design museums. – 27, 39, 198

Jasper Startup was born in London in 1961 and graduated with a degree in furniture design in 1983 from Middlesex Polytechnic. He received a Master of Arts degree in 1994 following an industrial design course at Central Saint Martin's College of Art and Design. Since 1983 he has worked freelance, designing for companies including Tangerine and Paul Priestman Associates. He has been a design tutor at Kingston University and at Central Saint Martin's, and from 1995 on the Foundation Studies course at Chelsea College of Art and Design. Since 1996 he has also held a seminar lectureship on design and environmentalism at Central Saint Martin's. – 89

Carouschka Streiffert is an architect, artist and stage-set designer. She was one of the leading figures behind the 'Stockholm Mobile' project in the 1980s. As a stage-designer she has collaborated with K. Kvarnström since 1990, creating sets for five major dance productions as well as an opera in Malmö. She has held shows throughout Europe, notably 'Plastic' which was exhibited at the Design Museum in London and the Kulturhuset in Stockholm. – 158

Stojanka Strugar was born in Yugoslavia and today works as an artist in England. She graduated from the Academy of Applied Arts in Belgrade in 1981, and received a diploma in textile design in 1984. Since then she has held numerous exhibitions in Yugoslavia and Europe. – 162

Shinichi Sumikawa was born in Tokyo in 1962 and graduated from the Industrial Design Department of Chiba University in 1984. Before establishing his own design studio in Tokyo he worked for Sony in Japan and the USA. He is a member of the Japan Industrial Designers' Association, and his work can be seen in the permanent collection of the National Technology of Science Museum, Ottawa, Canada. – 70

Ilkka Suppanen was born in 1968 in Kotka, Finland. He studied in the Faculty of Architecture at Helsinki University, at the University of Art and Design, Helsinki, and later at the Gerrit Rietveld Academy in Amsterdam. In 1995 he formed his own studio and since 1996 has taught at the University of Art and Design. He has exhibited at the Fifth International Exhibition of Architecture at the Venice Biennale, at the Island Gallery of Scandinavian Art in Den Haag, and in a touring exhibition from 1994–95 which travelled throughout Europe, Japan, Taiwan and Korea. He also took part in the 'Snowcrash' exhibition at the Gallery Facsimile during the 1997 Milan Furniture Fair. – 45, 55

Marco Susani and Mario Trimarchi are industrial designers who have been working together since 1986, developing household appliances, kitchen utensils, lamps, furniture and corporate identity schemes. Susani is director of the Domus Academy Research Centre in Milan, responsible for the Smart Tools Lab. His projects have been presented at the Milan Triennale; the Memphis Gallery, Milan; the Centre Georges Pompidou, Paris; the Axis Gallery, Tokyo; and the Grand Palais, Paris. Before joining Trimarchi he worked as one of the partners in Sottsass Associati and for the Olivetti Design Studio. Trimarchi is design consultant for Olivetti and also works in the studio of Michele de Lucchi where he is responsible for graphics, communication and art direction projects. From 1990–93 he was director of the Masters course in industrial design at the Domus Academy, where he still holds courses and seminars on industrial design. – 192

Svitalia Design was founded in 1986 by Susann Guempel and Urs Kamber. They have studios in Agra, Switzerland, and Milan. Guempel was born in 1956 in Germany and studied textile design in Basle. Kamber was born in 1948 in Switzerland, and studied architecture in Zurich, interior design in Basle and industrial design in Milan. The practice is involved in product design, interior decoration and interior architecture. Since 1989 Svitalia have manufactured under their own name, moving their head office to Ticino in Switzerland. Since 1990 they have moved into architectural projects. Both Guempel and Kamber lecture in design at the Istituto Europeo di Disegno, Milan, and Cagliari. – 74

Joe Tan is an industrial designer at IDEO, creating a variety of products for the consumer, computer, sports and medical industries. He studied product and transportation design in Europe, then product design at the Art Center College of Design in Pasedena, California. He received design excellence awards in 1994 and 1995. – 184

Shinkichi Tanaka was born in Fukuoka, Japan, in 1950 and graduated from the Kuwasawa Design School in 1972. He worked for Aiwa Co. Ltd before establishing Zero-One Design. His main clients are Sony, Aiwa, Kyosera, Windmill and Fujikowa Industry. He is a lecturer at the Kuwasawa Design School and a member of the Japan Industrial Designers' Association. – 181

Ilkka Terho see Valvomo Ltd

Mats Theselius was born in Stockholm in 1956. He studied industrial design at the National College of Art, Craft and Design, and today lives and works in Gothenburg. From 1979–94 he was involved in small-scale architectural projects in Sweden and the USSR, then became a professor at the HDK Industrial Design School in Gothenburg. He also works as an exhibition and interior designer. Examples of his work can be found in the Nationalmuseum, Stockholm; the Röhsska Museum, Gothenburg; the Malmö Museum, Copenhagen; and the Russian State Art Collection. – 196

Matteo Thun was born in 1952 in Bolzano, Italy, and studied at Florence University, then at the Academy of Oskar Kokoschka in Salzburg. Together with Ettore Sottsass he founded the Memphis group (1981) and Sottsass Associati. He is a prolific designer of ceramics and has worked as an architect for over 20 years. Since 1984 he has had his own design studio working for Bulgari, Alessi and Tiffany, amongst many other companies. His architectural work is concerned mainly with industrial and administrative buildings. – 82

Rud Thygesen received a diploma from the School of Art, Crafts and Design, Denmark, in 1966 and founded a design studio with Johnny Sørensen in the same year. The studio is active in furniture design, industrial design, graphics and textiles, with the main emphasis on furniture design for leading Danish companies. Thygesen's work can be found in the Danish Museum of Decorative Art, Copenhagen; the Nordenfjeldske Museum of Applied Art, Trondheim; the Oslo Museum of Applied Art; the Art Gallery and Museum of the Royal Pavilion, Brighton, England; the Victoria and Albert Museum, London; the Staatliches Museum für Angewandte Kunst, Munich; and the Museum of Modern Art, New York. – 46, 52, 71

Mario Trimarchi see Marco Susani

Oscar Tusquets Blanca was born in Barcelona in 1941. He attended the Escuela Técnica Superior de Arquitectura, Barcelona, and in 1964 established Studio Per with Lluis Clotet. They collaborated until 1984 when the company was dissolved and Bd Ediciones de Diseño was founded. In 1987 Tusquets set up Tusquets Diaz and Assoc. with Carlos Diaz to concentrate on architecture. He has been a guest professor and lecturer at universities in Germany, France and the USA, and awards for his work include the 'Creu de Sant Jordi' from the Autonomous Government of Catalonia; the National Award of Design; the Ciudad de Barcelona Award; and several FAD awards for architecture and Delta de Oro awards for design. In 1993 he received the Ardi-Montblanc award for best designer of the last five years. – 200

Andrew Tye was born in the UK in 1968. He studied three-dimensional design and furniture, and after working in a design studio for four years, established his own practice. Today his design pieces range from one-offs to production pieces. He has exhibited at '100% Design' in London and at other shows internationally. – 39

Valvomo Ltd is a group of eight young Finnish designers including Vesa Hinkola, Markus Nevalainen, Rane Vaskivuori, Ilkka Terho (senior partner and managing director) and Teppo Asikainen. They all studied architecture at the University of Technology in Helsinki and have exhibited their work in Finland, Denmark, and during the 1997 Milan Furniture Fair in the 'Snowcrash' exhibition at the Gallery Facsimile. – 42

Christine Van der Hurd was born in London and trained at Winchester College of Art. After graduating she designed textiles on a freelance basis for companies such as Kenzo, Cacherel, Mary Quant and Biba. She moved to the United States in 1976 and worked for Donghia and Jack Lenor Larson before setting up her own studio in 1980 and a Greenwich Village showroom in 1992. She designs a range of products from limited-edition carpets to decorative tapestries, cushions, accessories and glassware, but her specialization is in couture floor coverings commissioned to the specifications of architects and designers. In 1993 she began to create custom machine-made broadlooms in wool and nylon for larger residential and specialized contract use. – 159

Peter van der Jagt was born in 1971 in Doetinchem, The Netherlands. He studied at the Academy of Arts, Arnhem, and worked as a freelance designer in Amsterdam. He has exhibited his work at Droog Design/DMD shows in Milan, Amsterdam, Rotterdam, Copenhagen and Frankfurt. – 188, 190–1

Frans van Nieuwenborg was born in 1941 in Venio, The Netherlands. He studied at the Academy of Industrial Design in Eindhoven and throughout the 1970s was involved primarily in jewellery design and industrial products in small series, working with the designer Martijn Wegman. In 1986 he founded his own industrial design company and has since specialized in lighting. He has received international recognition for his work, including the Design Prize from the City of Rotterdam, and in 1994 participated in the IID'94 in Seoul, South Korea. – 80

Arnout Visser was born in 1962 and studied at the Art School in Arnhem, The Netherlands, from 1984–89, then at the Domus Academy, Milan, in 1990. Since then he has been working as a freelance designer in Arnhem, specializing in glass and ceramics. – 188, 190–1

Henk Vos was born in 1939 in The Netherlands and studied at the Academy of Design in Rotterdam from 1950–60. In 1963 he opened his own interior design office and furniture shop, designing mainly for Gelderland Meubelindustrie. In 1996 he founded a design store, Maupertuus, combined with a studio for industrial design and architecture run by his two sons Roderick and Bart. – 43

Roderick Vos was born in 1965 in The Netherlands and studied at the Academy of Industrial Design in Eindhoven from 1984–89. In 1990he founded a design studio, Maupertuus, with his wife, Claire Teevwen. He has exhibited his work at furniture fairs in the USA, Italy and The Netherlands. – 53

Bernard Vuarnesson trained as an engineer in the wood industry and started an office in Paris involved in calculating roof fabrics. In 1972 he founded Sculptures-Jeux and designed playground equipment with his wife, Ariana Vuarnesson. From 1975–80 he was a consultant at the Ecole Camondo, Paris. Today he designs interiors, furniture and products. – 102

Katie Walker studied furniture and related product design at Ravensbourne College of Design and Communication, Kent, England, and at the Royal College of Art, graduating as a Master of Arts in 1993. She founded Katie Walker Furniture with the support of a grant from the Crafts Council in 1994 and since then has received a number of private commissions and established a product line. – 61

Marcel Wanders graduated in product design from the Art Academy in Arnhem in 1988, by which time he had worked with Artifort and been awarded the Nestlé Design Prize. He was one of the founder members of WAAC Design and Consultancy, working with companies such as KLM, Swatch and Apple. In 1995 he opened his own studio, Wanders Wonders, and has broadened his client portfolio to include Cappellini, Rosenthal and British Airways. His work can be found in the permanent collections of the Stedelijk Museum, Amsterdam, and the Museum of Modern Art, New York. – 124

Norbert Wangen was born in Prüm, Germany. He served an apprenticeship as a carpenter from 1981–83, then studied architecture in Aachen and Munich, graduating as a certified engineer. Since 1991 he has designed stage sets for theatrical productions in Munich and Stuttgart and for the City Theatre in Landshut. He worked as a freelance designer for Riepl, Lauder and Wohr and for Gert Weber before founding his own company in 1994. He has exhibited at the Cologne, Milan and New York Furniture Fairs. – 58–9, 64

Weyers and Borms are self-taught designers. They began their collaboration in the 1980s and today are active in all areas of applied art from product design, logos and graphics to theatre, film-set and costume design. They often work with other artists to create one-off items for specific requests from clients, although some of their lights and textiles have been produced in limited batch numbers. They have exhibited their work throughout Europe. – 164

Ewa Wolk-Lewanowicz was born in Warsaw. She studied at the Fashion Institute of Technology in New York and later received a Masters degree from the Academy of Art in Warsaw. She designs interiors, stage sets, furniture, jewellery and costumes. – 29

Gerald Wurz studied mechanical engineering at the Federal College of Technology in Graz, Austria. He went on to train in architecture before undertaking a course in industrial design engineering at the Royal College of Art, London. He graduated as an industrial designer from the Hochschule für Angewandte Kunst in Vienna in 1993. During this period he was awarded the Stahlbaupreis, a national industrial design award, for his sun-shade project Solburch. His X-In Balance was shown at the Cologne Furniture Fair in 1997. – 209

YA/YA (Young Aspirations/Young Artists), is a collective of youth artists, founded in 1988. Located in New Orleans, it consists of 30 high-school and college students who work with Jana Napoli, the founder of YA/YA, and four other professional artists, developing their technical skills whilst producing work which reflects their culture and community. – 161

Manel Ybargüengoitia was born in Barcelona in 1954 and studied drawing and industrial design in Barcelona and Girona. He is a member of FAD, INFAD and the Official College of Decorators of Catalunya. – 94

Yellow Design, formally known as Team Industriform, was founded by Günter Horntrich in 1973 and is active in the fields of product planning, design development, modelling, industrial design, graphics and packaging. In 1992 the practice expanded to include Yellow Circle which carries out design studies and concepts and takes part in creative seminars and competitions. In the same year Horntrich became Professor for Ecology and Design at the Fachhochschule in Cologne. – 116

Thomas Zawalski founded the company Zaket in 1990. The Zaket collection includes both his own products and those of other members of his team. The Frankfurt Design-Plus award was given to Zawalski's Jo-Jo measuring tape in 1995. – 98, 210

Acerbis International SpA, Via Brusaporto 31, 24068 Seriate, Bergamo, Italy – Tel: (0)35 294222 – Fax: (0)35291454
Adelta, 96 Friedrich-Ebert-Strasse, D-46535 Dinslaken, Germany – Tel: (0)2064 40797 – Fax: (0)2064 40798
Alfa Romeo, Corso G. Agnelli, 10010 Torino, Italy – Tel: (0)11 6851111 – Fax: (0)11 6837591
Alessi SpA, Via Privata Alessi 6, Omegna 28026, Verbania VB, Italy – Tel: (0)323 868611 – Fax: (0)323 866132
Alias srl, Via dei Videtti 2, 24064 Grumello del Monte, Bergamo, Italy – Tel: (0)35 4420240 – Fax: (0)35 4420996
Alive Design, 28 Vendsysselvej, Vanløse 2720, Denmark – Tel: (0)31 87 78 57 – Fax: (0)31 87 78 57
Aluplus, 18 Mileparken, Skovlunde 2740, Denmark – Tel: (0)42 84 24 44 – Fax: (0)44 94 19 14
Amano Shikki Co. Ltd, 245 Haoka, Takaoka City 933, Toyama, Japan – Tel: (0)766 23 2151 – Fax: (0)766 25 6150
Menuiserie Anderegg SA, Olsenbachstrasse 7, 9631 Ulisbach/Toggenbourg, Switzerland – Tel: (0)74 7 12 36 – Fax: (0)74 712 53
Andreu World SA, Camino de los Mojones /km. 2,500, Alaquas 46970, Valencia, Spain – Tel: (0)6 150 21 50 – Fax: (0)6 150 22 77
Antworks, 81 Vale Street, Moorooka 4105, Queensland, Australia – Tel: (0)7 3892 4184 – Fax: (0) 7 3892 4184
Aqua Creations, 69 Maze, Tel Aviv 65789, Israel – Tel: (0)3 5602197 – Fax: (0)3 560 7756
Arcade, Via Goethe 2, Bolzano 39100, Italy – Tel: (0)471 980 795 – Fax: (0)471 977 592
Arper, c/o Feltrin & Radcliffe, Via Callalta 99/a, 31057 Silea (TV), Italy – Tel: (0)422 362638/361152 – Fax: (0)422 362642
Art & Design, 1 Molenstraat, B-3630 Maasmechelen, Belgium – Tel: (0)89 757968 – Fax: (0)89 757968
Artel Ltd, 1555 Libensky Ostrov, Prague 8, 180 00, Czech Republic – Tel: (0)2 683 3685 – Fax: (0)2 683 3685
Asplund, 31 Sibyllegatan, Stockholm 11442, Sweden – Tel: (0)8 662 5284 – Fax: (0)8 662 3885
Atelier Alinea AG, Zähringerstrasse 14, CH-4007 Basle, Switzerland – Tel: (0)61 690 97 97 – Fax: (0)61 690 97 90
Atlantis, Via LaValle, 220676 Mariano Comense (CO), Italy – Tel: (0)31 75 11 91 – Fax: (0)31 74 47 16
Audi AG, 85045 Ingolstadt, Germany – Tel: (0)841 89 40 82 – Fax: (0)841 8992373
Authentics, 30 Max-Eyth-Strasse, Holzgerlingen 71088, Germany – Tel: (0)7031 68 05 0 – Fax: (0)7031 68 05 99
Masayo Ave, Via Disciplini 5, Milan 20123, Italy
Azumi's/S.Planning Co., Ground Floor, 953 Finchley Road, London NW11 7PE, UK – Tel: (0)181 731 7496 – Fax: (0)181 731 7496

BayGen Power Europe Ltd, Claverton House, Longwood Court, Love Lane, Cirencester, Glos. GL7 1YG, UK –
Tel: (0)1285 65 9559 – Fax: (0)1285 65 9550
Bd Ediciones de Diseño SA, 291 Mallorca, Barcelona 08037, Spain – Tel: (0)3 458 69 09 – Fax: (0)3 207 36 97
Biesse SpA, Via Nobel 43, Lissone 20035, (MI), Italy – Tel: (0)39 484322 – Fax: (0)39 481812
Bimota, Via Giaccaglia 38, 47037 Rimini, Italy – Tel: (0)541 383493 – Fax: (0)541 383259
Bisque, 244 Belsize Road, London NW6 4BT, UK – Tel: (0)171 328 2225 – Fax: (0)171 328 9845
Blauet SA, 333 Aragon, Barcelona 08008, Spain – Tel: (0)3 207 53 11 – Fax: (0)3 207 33 98
B.Lux SA, s/n Poligono Eitua, Berriz 48240, Vizcaya, Spain – Tel: (0)4 682 7272 – Fax: (0)4 682 4902
Julie Blyfield, 10 Sydney Place, Adelaide, South Australia – Fax: (0) 8 8223 6089
Renata Bonfanti Snc, Via Piana d'Oriente 52, Mussolente 36065, Vicenza, Italy – Tel: (0)424 577008 – Fax: (0)424 577008
Borås Cotton AB, Box 52, Borås S-503 06, Sweden – Tel: (0)33 170300 – Fax: (0)33 136778

CableVision, 41 Postweg, D-73079 Süssen, Germany – Tel: (0)7162 400784 – Fax: (0)7162 41441
Campeggi srl, Via del Cavolto 8, 22040 Anzano del Parco (Como), Italy – Tel: (0)31 630495 – Fax: (0)31 632205
Design Center Canon Inc., 3-30-2 Shimomaruko, Ohta-ku 146, Tokyo, Japan – Tel: (0)3 3758 2111 – Fax: (0)3 3758 9852
Caroline Casey Design, Level 1, 63 William Street, East Sydney 2010, Australia – Tel: (0)2 9360 2322 – Fax: (0)2 9360 2123
Casanostra AG, Felsenstrasse 34a, CH-9000 St Gallen, Switzerland – Tel: (0)71 222 98 11 – Fax: (0)71 222 98 12
cbi, Birger Jarlsgatan 34, Box 26126, S-100 41 Stockholm, Sweden – Tel: (0)8 611 5252 – Fax: (0)8 611 7565
Chubu Design Research Center Co. Ltd, 1-3-20 Dekimachi, Nagoya 461, Aichi, Japan – Tel: (0)52 931 6804 – Fax: (0)52 932 2215
ClassiCon GmbH, 8 Perchtinger Strasse, 81379 Munich, Germany – Tel: (0)89 74 81 33-0 – Fax: (0)89 7 80 99 96
Cleverline, 10 Zuidlaardermeer, Rotterdam 3068 KL, The Netherlands – Tel: (0)10 2071200 – Fax: (0)10 4213872
Colombo Design SpA, Via Baccanello 22, Terno D'Isola 24030 (BG), Italy – Tel: (0)35 905475 – Fax: (0)35 4940257
Concord Lighting Ltd, Avis Way, Newhaven, East Sussex BN9 OED, UK – Tel: (0)1273 515811 – Fax: (0)1273 611014
Costantino, c/o Ardes, Via Lombardia 71, 74100 Taranto, Italy – Tel: (0)99 73 67 789 – Fax: (0)99 73 82 380

D Line International AS, 28 Carl Jacobsensvej, Copenhagen 1790, Denmark. – Tel: (0)36 18 04 00
Danish Technological Institute, Gregersvej, Taastrup 2630, Denmark – Tel: (0)43 504350 – Fax: (0)43 507250
Chanan de-Lange, 20 Refidim St., Tel Aviv 69982, Israel – Fax: (0)3 647 1914
Design Ideas, PO Box 2967, Springfield, Illinois 62708, USA – Tel: (0)217 753 3081 – Fax: (0)217 753 3080
Designum, 2 Julianalaan 2, Laag Keppel 6998 AR., The Netherlands – Tel: (0)314 381396 – Fax: (0)314 382286
Gabriele de Vecchi, Via Lombardini 20, Milan 20143, Italy – Tel: (0)2 8323 365 – Fax: Milan (0)2 58101 174
Jos Devriendt, Belgradostr. 87, Ghent 9000, Belgium
David D'Imperio, 2961 Aviation Avenue, Miami 33133, Florida, USA – Tel: (0)305 285 1298 – Fax: (0)305 285 1130
Di(Sain) Hagn & Kubala OEG, 69 Zieglergasse, Vienna 1070, Austria – Tel: (0)1 522 22 55 – Fax: (0)1 522 22 56
DNR Sportsystem Ltd, 32 Mühlebachstrasse, Zurich 8032, Switzerland – Tel: (0)1 266 51 30 – Fax: (0)1 266 51 60
DPG Ltd (The Design and Production Group), The Hat Factory, 16-18 Hollen Street, Soho, London W1V 3AD, UK –
Tel: (0)171 437 5060 – Fax: (0)171 437 5070
Driade, Via Ancona 1/1, Milan 20121, Italy – Tel: (0) 2 72023203 – Fax: (0) 2 72002434
Droog Design, Keizerssgracht 518, 1017 EK Amsterdam, The Netherlands – Tel: (0)31 20 63 82 986 – Fax: (0)31 20 63 88 828

Edra Mazzei, PO Box 28, 56030 Perignano (PI), Italy – Tel: (0)587 616660 – Fax: (0)587 617500
Thomas Eisl, 3 Nimrod Passage, London N1 4BU, UK
Elam, Via Molino 27, 20036 Meda, Milan, Italy – Tel: (0)362 73781 – Fax: (0)362 340522.
Electrolux Zanussi Elettrodomestici SpA, Via G. Cattaneo 3, Pordenone 33170, (PN), Italy – Tel: (0)434 396210 – Fax: (0)434 396045
EmmeBi e la Notte, Via Monteverdi 28, 20031 Cesano Maderno, Milan, Italy – Tel: (0)362 502296/552274 – Fax: (0)362 509602
Everyday Design, 38 Kulosaaren Puistotie, Helsinki 00570, Finland – Tel: (0)40 5476565 – Fax: (0)9 6211636

F. Fabbian & F.lli Snc, Via S. Brigida 50, Resana 31020, Treviso, Italy – Tel: (0)423 784535/6/7 – Fax: (0)423 484395
Fasem, c/o Relazioni Pubbliche Azioni Privilegiate srl, Via D'Annunzio 227, 50135 Florence, Italy –
Tel: (0)55 69 79 46 – Fax: (0)55 69 78 56
Fedra BV, Via Soave 8, Lugano 6900, Switzerland – Tel: (0)91 9210562 – Fax: (0)91 9210564
Feldmann & Schultchen, 7 Timmermannstrasse, D-22299 Hamburg, Germany – Tel: (0)40 51 0000 – Fax: (0)40 51 7000
Ferrari SpA, Via Abetone Inferiore 4, 41053 Maranello (MO), Italy – Tel: (0)536 949111 – Fax: (0)536 941161
Fiat Auto SpA, Corso G. Agnelli, 10010 Torino, Italy – Tel: (0)11 6851111 – Fax: (0)11 6837591
Flos SpA, Via Angelo Faini 2, 25073 Bovezzo Brescia, Italy – Tel: (0)30 2712161-2438.1 – Fax: (0)30 2711578
Ford Motor Co. Ltd., Central Office, Eagle Way, Brentwood, Essex, UK – Tel: (0)1277 253000 – Fax: (0)1277 253020
Foster and Partners, Riverside Three, 22 Hester Road, London SW11 4AN, UK – Tel: (0)171 738 0455 – Fax: (0)171 738 1107/8
Henrik Frederiksen, Frederik V Svej 17, Copenhagen 2100, Denmark – Fax: (0)3 5433209.
Fritz Moebel, 5 Am Mittelberg, Rosrath 51503, Germany – Tel: (0)2205 82895 – Fax: (0)2207 3461
Front Corporation, 3-13-1 Takadanobaba, Shinjuku-ku 169, Tokyo, Japan – Tel: (0)3 3360 3391 – Fax: (0)3 3362 6363

Fujikowa Industry Co. Ltd, 3-23-3 Shinmachi, Setagaya 154, Tokyo, Japan – Tel: (0)3 5477 6601 – Fax: (0)3 5477 6618

Garcia Garay SL, 13 San Antonio, Sta. Coloma Gnt 08923, Barcelona, Spain – Tel: (0)3 466 10 16 – Fax: (0)3 386 23 72
Gelderland Furniture, Postbus 13, 4100AA Culemborg - 7 Stationsweg, Culemborg 4101 N6, Gelderland, Holland –
Tel: (0)345 512841 – Fax: (0)345 518184
General Binding Corporation, 1 GBC Plaza, Northbrook, IL 60062, USA – Tel: (0)847 272 3700
GH Form, 22 Lundemarksvej, Holbaeck 4300, Denmark – Tel: (0)53 43 0413.
Nuala Goodman, Via Cagnola 7, 20154 Milan, Italy – Fax: (0)2 33104187
Goods, 218 Prinsengracht, Amsterdam 1016 HD, Holland – Tel: (0)20 6385908 – Fax: (0)20 6204457
Tobias Grau KG GmbH & Co., 18 Borselstrasse, 22765 Hamburg, Germany – Tel: (0)40 391655 – Fax: (0)40 392144
Atelier Greter AG, Seefeldstrasse 223, CH-8008 Zurich, Switzerland – Tel: (0)1 381 34 47 – Fax: (0)1 381 34 49

Hamax As, Makeveien 4, N-1679 Krakeroy, Norway – Tel: (0)69 34 00 33 – Fax: (0)69 34 22 73
Fritz Hansen A/S, 8 Allerødvej, Allerød 3450, Denmark – Tel: (0)48 17 23 00 – Fax: (0)48 17 19 48
Noa Hanyu, 979 Nakaotsuda Miyashita, Mishima-machi, Onuma-Gun, Fukushima, Japan
Helix-Akantus, 371 Hammer Strasse, Münster 48153, Germany
Herbst LaZar Bell Inc., 355 N. Canal Street, Chicago, IL 60606, USA – Tel: (0)312 454 1116 – Fax: (0)312 454 9019
Helena Hernmarck Tapestries, 879 North Salem Road, Ridgefield, CT 06877, USA – Tel: (0)203 431 9570
Knud Holscher Industrial Design, Vermundsgade 40, 2100 Copenhagen, Denmark – Tel: (0)39 29 10 01 – Fax: (0)39 29 67 01
Horas International, 25 Beemdstraat, Ruisbroek, Brussels B-1601, Belgium – Tel: (0)2 3348450 – Fax: (0)2 3781622
David Huycke, 160 Bekelstraat, Sint-Niklaas 9100, Belgium – Tel: (0)3 776 89 58 – Fax: (0)3 766 56 12

Iduna srl, Via Solferino 27, Milan 20121, Italy – Tel: (0)2 655498/95 – Fax: (0)2 29011311
iGuzzini Illuminazione, S.S 77, Recanati 62019, Macerata 071, Italy – Tel: (0)71 75881 – Fax: (0)71 7588295
Iittala Glass, Hackman Designor Oy, Hämeentie 135, Iittala 14500, Finland – Tel: (0)204 39 6231 – Fax: (0)204 39 6283
Inflate, 5 Old Street, London EC1V 9HL, UK – Tel: (0)171 251 5453 – Fax: (0)171 250 0311
In House, Higashi Building 31, 21-15-7 Nishi-Azabu, Minato-ku 106, Japan – Tel: (0)3 3498 9811 – Fax: (3) 3498 9801
Interier Maly, 6 Marákova, Prague 160 00, Czech Republic – Tel: (0)422 320403 – Fax: (0)422 32043
Interlübke GmbH & Co. KG, 145 Ringstrasse, D-33378 Rheda-Widenbruck, Germany – Tel: (0)5242 12-1 – Fax: (0)5242 12-206
Italiana Luce srl, Via Edison 118, Settimo Milanese 20019, Italy – Tel: (0)2 48915671 – Fax: (0)2 48910561
Setsu Ito, Via F. Filzi 5, Milan, Italy – Fax: (0)2 67071495

Feliksas Jakubauskas, 7-2 Sv. Jono, Vilnius 2001, Lithuania – Fax: (0)3702 222 888
Jo-el A/S, Orbaekvej 280, DK-5220, Odense 5220, Denmark – Tel: (0)63 151000 – Fax: (0)63 151055
JVC Design Center, 3-12 Moriya-cho, Kanagawa-ku 221, Yokohama, Japan – Tel: (0)45 450 2431 – Fax: (0)45 450 2441

Källemo AB, 30 Växjövägen, Värnamo S-331 26, Sweden – Tel: (0)370 150 00 – Fax: (0)370 150 60
Kartell SpA, Via delle Industrie 1, 20082 Noviglio (Milano), Italy – Tel: (0)2 90012.1 – Fax: (0)2 9053316
Kautzky Mechanik GsmbH, Schöffelgasse 28-28, Vienna A-1180, Austria
Sirkka Könönen, Liisankatu 17A, PL 326, 00171 Helsinki, Finland
Kotzolt Leuchten, 72-76a Lagesche Strasse, Lemgo 32657, Germany – Tel: (0)5261 2190 – Fax: (0)5261 5261
Kron SA, s/n Camino Ancho, Daganzo 28814, Madrid, Spain – Tel: (0)1 884 52 60 – Fax: (0)1 884 13 92
Kundalini srl, Via Plutarco 6, Milan 20145, Italy – Tel: (0)2 468244/4989587 – Fax: (0)2 48194560

Lampert & Sudrow GmbH & Co. KG, 12b Gaisburgstrasse, D-70182 Stuttgart, Germany – Tel: (0)711 234 8008 – Fax: (0)711 234 8007
Lantal Textiles, 5 Dorfgasse, Langenthal, CH-4901, Switzerland – Tel: (0)62 916 71 71 – Fax: (0)62 923 25 32
Larsen Design, 233 Spring Street, New York, NY 10013, USA – Tel: (0)212 462 1300 – Fax: (0)212 462 1307
Leclanche SA, 48 Av. de Grandson, Yverdon-les-Bains 1401, Switzerland – Tel: (0)24 447 22 72 – Fax: (0)24 445 24 42
Ewa Wolk Lewanowicz, c/o Alicja Trusiewicz, ul. Mielczarskiego 1/82, 02-798 Warsaw, Poland –
Tel: (0)22 648 25 33 – Fax: (0)22 648 25 33
Christianna Los, Red Cow Studios, Larnaca Works, Grange Walk, London SE1 3AG, UK – Tel: (0)171 237 9360
Lucitalia SpA, Via P. Da Volpedo 50, Cinisello B. Mo. 20092, Milan, Italy – Tel: (0)2 86461250/6126651 – Fax: (0)2 874990

Magis srl, Via Magnadola 15, 31045 Motta di Livenza (Treviso), Italy – Tel: (0)422 768742 – Fax: (0)422 766395
Magnus Olesen, Agertoft 2, Durup, Postbox 131, DK-7870 Roslev, Denmark – Tel: (0)97 59 24 11 – Fax: (0)97 59 29 22
Marset Iluminación SA, 429 Alfonso XII, Badalona 08912, Barcelona, Spain – Tel:(0)3 460 01 07 – Fax: (0)3 460 10 89
Jonathan Marshall, c/o Studio X, 21 Powis Mews, London W11 1JN, UK – Fax: (0)171 229 7032
Matsushita Electric Industrial Co. Ltd, 2-15 Matsuba-cho, Kadoma, Osaka 571, Japan – Tel: (0)6 905 4687 – Fax: (0)6 905 4048
Maupertuus, 41 Ubbo-Emmiussingel, Groningen 9711BC, Groningen, Holland – Tel: (0)50 3181212/5244244 – Fax: (0)50 5244255
Ingo Maurer GmbH, 47 Kaiserstrasse, Munich 80801, Germany – Tel: (0)89 3816060 – Fax: (0)89 38160620
Mauser Enrichtungen AG, Wildinger Landstrasse, Waldeck D-3544, Germany – Tel: (0)5623 581346 – Fax: (0)5623 581300
Meinecke Collection, 1 East Delaware, Chicago, Illinois 60611, USA – Tel: (0)312 787 4504 – Fax: (0)312 787 4942
Mercedes Benz AG, Presse 70322, Stuttgart, Germany – Tel: (0)711 17-0 – Fax: (0)711 17 222 44.
Messenger Service, 2 Slabky, Prague 180 00, Czech Republic – Tel: (0)2 6836323 – Fax: (0)2 6836323
Metz Schlett Kindler, 44 Frankfurter Strasse, Darmstadt 64293, Germany – Tel: (0)6151 293641 – Fax: (0)6151 295252
Minox GmbH, 4 Walter-Zapp-Strasse, Wetzlar 35578, Germany – Tel: (0)6441 917-0 – Fax: (0)6441 917-601
Montis, Steenstraat 2, Postbus 153, 5100 AD Dongen, Holland – Tel: (0)162 377777 – Fax: (0)162 377710
Moormann Möbel– und Handels GmbH, Kirchplatz, Aschau/Chiemgau 83229, Germany – Tel: (0)8052 4001 – Fax: (0)8052 4393

Namaste Handels, 104 Schirmerweg, Munich 81247, Germany – Tel: (0)89 811 75 34 – Fax: (0)89 8145117
Naos srl, Via O. Rosai 1, Figline Valdarno 50063 (FI), Italy – Tel: (0)55 96 14 61 – Fax: (0)55 96 16 90
Mikala Naur, 37 GL Mønt, Copenhagen 1117 K, Denmark – Fax: (0)39 27 44 40
Nava Design SpA, Via Martin Lutero 5, Milan 20126, (MI), Italy – Tel: (0)2570251 – Fax: (0)26300518
N/P/K Industrial Design, Noordeinde 2d, 2311 CD Leiden, The Netherlands – Tel: (0)71 5141341 – Fax: (0)71 5130410
N2, Postfach 6330, 6000 Lucerne 6, Switzerland – Tel: (0)61 693 4011 – Fax: (0)61 693 4015
Oy Netsurfer Ltd, Korppaanmäentie 21A, 00300 Helsinki, Finland – Tel: (0)9 241 0212 – Fax: (0)9 241 0218.
Neudorf Ceramics, RD2 Neudorf Road, Upper Moutere, Nelson, New Zealand – Tel: (0)3 5432640 – Fax: (0)3 5432640
New Leucos SpA, Via Treviso 77, Scorze 33037, Venice, Italy – Tel: (0)41 5859111 – Fax: (0)41 447598
Niewiadomski Industrial Design, 32 Bandwirkerstrasse, D-22041 Hamburg, Germany – Tel: (0)40 68 69 60 – Fax: (0)40 68 69 60
Norton Healthcare, Gemini House, Flex Meadow, Harlow, Essex CM19 5TJ, UK – Tel: (0)1279 426666 – Fax: (0)1279 432110
Nova Form, 6 Färbergasse, A-8010 Graz, Austria – Tel: (0)664 2107 805 – Fax: (0)316 8222 637
Novito, 404 Lukesova, Steti 411 08, Czech Republic – Tel: (0)411 500 472
nya nordiska, An den Ratswiesen, D-29451 Dannenberg, Germany – Tel: (0)5861 8090 – Fax: (0)5861 80912

Oken SA, Sr. Joan Tó, Strauss s/n, Poligono Industrial Can Jardi, Rubi 08191, Barcelona, Spain –
Tel: (0)3 588 25 68 – Fax: (0)3 588 03 45
O.L.A.L.A, 5 Brunhildstrasse, Berlin 10829, Germany – Tel: (0)30 7829973 – Fax: (0)30 2828532
Olgoj Chorchoj, 1555 Libensky Ostrov, Prague 8, 180 00, Czech Republic – Tel: (0)2 6833685 – Fax: (0)2 6833685
Olivetti Lexikon SpA, Jervis 77, Ivrea 10015, Torino, Italy – Tel: (0)125 52 00
Olympus Optical Co. (Europa) GmbH, 14-16 Wendenstrasse, 20097 Hamburg, Postfach 10 49 08, 20034 Hamburg, Germany –
Tel: (0)40 2 37 73 0. – Fax: (0)40 23 08 17
Opus Magnum (David Field), 313 Merton Road, London SW18, UK – Tel: (0)181 332 2449 – Fax: (0)181 332 2393
Orrefors – Kosta Boda AB, Orrefors 38040, Sweden – Tel: (0)481 3400 – Fax: (0)481 30350

Parker Pen Company, Parker House, Newhaven, East Sussex BN9 0AU, UK – Tel: (0)1273 513289 – Fax: (0)1273 513589
UMS-Pastoe BV, EM Albers, Rotsoord 3, Utrecht 3523 CL, Holland – Tel: (0)30 258 55 55 – Fax: (0)30 252 23 40
Stefan Patte Design, 30 Hellabrunner Strasse, Munich 81543, Germany – Tel: (0)89 657867 – Fax: (0)89 657868
P. & L. Pelechov, Pelechov, Czech Republic – Tel: (0)428 389334 – Fax: (0)428 389292
Stephen Philips Design UK, 71 Sheepfold Road, Guildford, Surrey GU2 6TU, UK – Tel: (0)1483 566545 – Fax: (0)1483 566545
Poliform SpA, Via Montesanto 28, Inverigo 22044, Como, Italy – Tel: (0)31 6951 – Fax: (0)31 699444
Poltrona Frau srl, SS 77km 75.5, Tolentino I-62029 (MC), Italy – Tel: (0)733 90 91 – Fax: (0)733 971600
Polycom, 2854 Junction Avenue, San Jose, CA 95134, USA.
Proactiv, 38/1 Hauptstrasse, Dotternhausen 72359, Germany – Tel: (0)7427 2239 – Fax: (0)7427 7374
Procter-Rihl, Spatial Interference, 190c Royal College Street, London NW1 9NN, UK – Tel: (0)171 284 0248 – Fax: (0)171 916 1517
Produzione Privata, Via Pallavicino 31, Milan 20145, Italy – Tel: (0)2 43008302 – Fax: (0)2 43008222
Punt Mobles SL, 48 Islas Baleares, Fuente del Jarro 46988, Valencia, Spain – Tel: (0)6 1320013 – Fax: (0)6 1320287

Raffelberg Kollektion, 68 Graurheindorfer Strasse, Bonn 53111, Germany – Tel: (0)228 985310 – Fax: (0)228 9853116
Rexite SpA, Via Edison 7, 20090 Cusago, Milan, Italy – Tel: (0)2 90390013 – Fax: (0)2 90390018
Ribag Licht AG, 1 Kesslerstrasse, CH-5037 Muhen, Switzerland – Tel: (0)62 737 90 10 – Fax: (0)62 737 90 18
Ann Richards, 16 Albany Road, Southsea, Hants. PO5 2AB, UK
Robots SpA, Via Galvahi 7, Binasco 20082, Milan, Italy – Tel: (0)2 9054661 – Fax: (0)2 9054664.
Vibeke Rohland, 19 Holbergsgade, Copenhagen DK-1057, Denmark – Tel: (0)33 91 00 44 – Fax: (0)33 14 44 06
T.P. Rond srl, 27 Vle Bligny, Milan 20136, Italy – Tel: (0)2 58314543 – Fax: (0)2 58319980
Rosenthal AG, 43 Wittelsbacherstrasse, Selb 95100, Germany – Tel: (0)9287 72566 – Fax: (0)9287 72271
Roset SA, BP 9, Briord 01470, France – Tel: (0)4 74 36 17 00 – Fax: (0)4 74 36 12 92
Röthlisberger Schreinerei AG, Dorfstrasse 73, CH-3073 Gümligen, Switzerland – Tel: (0)31 951 41 17 – Fax: (0)31 951 75 64
Royal Copenhagen, 45 Smallegade, Copenhagen DK-2000, Denmark – Tel: (0)31 86 48 48 – Fax: (0)31 86 30 13

Sabattini Argenteria srl, Don Capiaghi 2, Bregnano 22070, Como, Italy – Tel: (0)31 771019 – Fax: (0)31 773386
Sabrina Creative Productions, Viale Kennedy 10, Bregnano 22070, Como, Italy – Tel: (0)31 773473 – Fax: (0)31 773473
Sahco Hesslein GmbH, 17-19 Kreuzburger Strasse, Nürnberg D-90471, Germany – Tel: (0)911 99870 – Fax: (0)911 9987480
Sakaegi Design Studio, 1-74 Nakamizuno-cho, Seto-shi 489, Aichi-ken, Japan – Tel: (0)561 48 3991 – Fax: (0)561 48 3991
Timo Salli, Muotoilutoimisto Salli, Meritullinkatu 11, 00170 Helsinki, Finland – Tel: (0)9 2782277 – Fax: (0)9 2782277
Kasper Salto, 26c Ostergade, Copenhagen 1453, Denmark – Fax: (0)33 32 27 80
Hector Santos, Pi Design, 13620 Imperial Highway No. 5, Santa Fe Springs, CA 90670-4842, USA – Tel: (0)562 407 1590
Sawaya & Moroni SpA, Via Andegari 18, Milan 20121, Italy – Tel: (0)2 863951 – Fax: (0)2 86464831
Schmidinger Modul Wohn & Objektbedarf GmbH, 146 Stangenach, Schwarzenberg A-6867, Vorarlberg, Austria –
Tel: (0)5512 2782 14 – Fax: (0)5512 2782 2
Schulte Design, 59 Marktstrasse, Krefeld D-47798, Germany – Tel: (0)2151 625910 – Fax: (0)2151 625920
Sculptures-Jeux, 18 rue Dornat, Paris 75005, France – Tel: (0)1 43 54 20 39 – Fax: (0)1 43 54 83 32
Sellex, Apartado 273, 20080 San Sebastian, Donosti Ibilbidea 84, Poligono 26 – 20115 Astigarraga, Spain –
Tel: (0)43 55 70 11/55 74 00 – Fax: (0)43 55 70 50/55 75 50
Serafino Zani, Via Zanagnolo 17b, Lumezzane 25066 (BS), Italy – Tel: (0)30 871861 – Fax: (0)30 872545
John and Penny Smith, 502 Nelson Road, Mt Nelson, Hobart 7007, Tasmania, Australia – Fax: (0)3 62 264308
Jasper Startup, Unit F6, The Chocolate Factory, Farleigh Place, London N16 7SX, UK – Tel: (0)171 503 5344 – Fax: (0)171 503 5344
Steklarska Sola, 1 Steklarska Ulica, Rogaska Slatina, Slovenia – Tel: (0)38663 814 911 – Fax: (0)38663 814 616
Stojanka Strugar, 73 Eton Avenue, London NW3 3EU, UK
Studio D (Ralph Ball), Studio D, Hatcham PK Mews Centre, London SE14, UK – Tel: (0) 171 639 1639
Studio Ilkka Suppanen Oy, Pohjoisranta 8E 104, 00170 Helsinki, Finland – Tel: (0)9 6223093 – Fax: (0)9 6223093
Svitalia, Piazzetta, Agra 6927, Ticino, Switzerland – Tel: (0)91 9943345 – Fax: (0)91 9946561

TKO, 20 Northampton Square, London EC1V 0AJ, UK – Tel: (0)171 490 2505 – Fax: (0)171 490 2502
Toshiba Corporation Design Center, 1-1 Shibaura 1-cho-me, Minato-ku, Tokyo 105-01, Japan – Tel: (0)3 3457 4020 – Fax: (0)3 5444 9291
Transglass, Studio 16, 33 Rushworth Street, London SE1 0RB, UK – Tel: (0)171 261 9315 – Fax: (0)171 277 8394
2.5 Dimensional Design x Tsujiyo, 17-2 Uzumachi, Isahaya 854, Nagasaki, Japan – Tel: (0)957 24 2371 – Fax: (0)957 62 8663
Tye, 104 Oxo Tower Wharf, Bargehouse Street, London SE1 9PH, UK – Tel: (0)171 633 9001 – Fax: (0)171 928 5000

Umbra, 2358 Midland Avenue, Scarborough, Ontario M1S 1P8, Canada – Tel: (0)416 299 0088 – Fax: (0)416 299 6168
Unifor SpA, Via Isonzo 1, Turate 22078, Como, Italy – Tel: (0)2 967191 – Fax: (0)2 96750859
Unique Interieur, 4 Kalkbraenderilobskaj, Copenhagen DK-2100, Denmark – Tel: (0)31 200233 – Fax: (0)31 200256
U-X Umwelt-Exploratorium, 2 Elsenbornerstrasse, Frankfurt 65929, Germany

Valli and Valli, Via Concordia 16, Renate 20055, Italy – Tel: (0)362 982271 – Fax: (0)362 982214
Valvomo Ltd, Uudenmaankatu 33E, 00120 Helsinki, Finland – Tel: (0)9 68033887 – Fax: (0)9 611269.
Christine Van der Hurd, c/o Susan Harkavy, 201 W 70 No. 2B, New York, NY 10023, USA – Tel: (0)212 873 4687
Van Nieuwenborg Industrial Design Consultancy Group, 99c Plantsoen, Leiden 2311 KL, The Netherlands –
Tel: (0)31 5123230 – Fax: (0)31 5131587
Michele Veccia Edizioni Design, Via dei Macci 24r, 50122 Florence, Italy – Tel: (0)55 2480057 – Fax: (0)55 2480057
Vitra (International) AG, 22 Klünenfeldstrasse, Birsfelden 4127, Switzerland – Tel: (0)61 315 15 09 – Fax: (0)61 316 15 10
VOKO, 4-10 Am Pfahlgraben, Pohlheim 35415, Germany – Tel: (0)604 929-0/279 – Fax: (0)604 929 615
Volkswagen AG, Wolfsburg, D-38436, Germany – Tel: (0)5361 9-0 – Fax: (0)5361 9-2 82 82
Gebr. vom Braucke GmbH & Co., 05 Telgenbrink, Bielefeld 22739, Germany – Tel: (0)521 8001-0 – Fax: (0)521 8001-180
VS Vereinigte Spezialmöbelfabriken GmbH & Co., 8 Hochhäuser Strasse, Tauberbischofsheim 97941, Germany –
Tel: (0)9341 880 – Fax: (0)9341 88107

Katie Walker Furniture, Cox Farm Studios, Dorking Road, Warnham RH12 3RZ, West Sussex, UK –
Tel: (0)1403 211323 – Fax: (0)1403 211323
Norbert Wangen, 6 Grafinger Strasse, D-81671, Munich, Germany – Tel: (0)89 49 00 15 72 – Fax: (0)89 49 00 15 73
Watch People, Schöll & Brassler GmbH, 29a Pfingstrosenstrasse, Munich D-81377, Germany –
Tel: (0)89 719 2033 – Fax: (0)89 719 5499.
Weyers & Borms, Antwerpse Steenweg 48, 9140 Tielrode, Belgium – Tel: (0)3 7110517 – Fax: (0)3 7111947
Wilkhahn, Postfach 2070, D-31844, Bad Münder, Germany – Tel: (0)5042 999263/96 – Fax: (0)5042 999130
A. Winther A/S, Rygesmindevej 2, DK 8653 Them, Denmark – Tel: (0)86 84 72 88 – Fax: (0)86 84 85 28
W.M.F. AG, Eberhardstrasse, Geislingen D-73312, Steige, Germany – Tel: (0)331 251 – Fax: (0)331 45387

XO, Cide 4-Servon, Brie Comte Robert 77170, France – Tel: (0)1 64 05 54 98 – Fax: (0)1 64 05 54 94

YA/YA Young Aspirations/Young Artists Inc., 628 Baronne Street, New Orleans, LA, USA –
Tel: (0)504 529 3306 – Fax: (0)504 529 7432
Yamada Shomei Lighting Co. Inc., 3-16-12 Sotokanda, Chiyoda-ku, Tokyo 101, Japan
Yamaha Corporation, 10-1, Nakazawa-cho, Shizuoka 430, Japan – Tel: (0)53 460 2883 – Fax: (0)53 463 4922

Zaket Haus & Wohnen Vertreib GmbH, 15 Seelandstrasse, Lübeck 23569, Germany – Tel: (0)451 3909130 – Fax: (0)451 3909110
Zani & Zani, Via del Porto 51/53m 25088 Toscalano (BS), Italy – Tel: (0)365 641 006/644 281 – Fax: (0)365 644 281
Zanotta SpA, Via Vittorio Veneto 57, Nova Milanese 20054, Milan, Italy – Tel: (0)362 368330 – Fax: (0)362 451038
Zero One Design, Jinnan Heim, 1/4/2/ Jinnan, Shibuya-ku, Tokyo 150, Japan – Tel: (0)3 3464 0035 – Fax: (0)3 3496 0588
Zumtobel Licht GmbH, 30 Schweizerstrasse, Dornbirn 6850, Vorarlberg, Austria – Tel: (0)5572 390 636 – Fax: (0)5572 390 182

Acquisitions by design collections in 1997.
Dates given in parentheses refer to the dates of the designs
(from 1960 to the present day).

AUSTRALIA
Powerhouse Museum, Sydney, New South Wales

Auto Union GmbH s car, Audi 200 Turbo (1986)
Robert Baines silver and titanium teaset, Waikato (1989, 1995)
Ada Bird Petyarre textile length of Australian bush designs (1995), manufactured by Utopia Awley Batik
Christopher Connell chair, Pepe (1990–92), manufactured by MAP
Stuart Devlin knife and scabbard, Wiltshire Staysharp MK1 (1969), manufactured by McPherson's Homewares
Alex Issigonis motor car, Leyland Mini K (1959), manufactured by Leyland Australia (1970)
Ruth McDermott and Rina Bernabei electric light fitting, Bernini Lights Up (1996), manufactured by Ovo Design
Karl Millard pepper grinder, Bulbous (1996)
Gerry Mussett and Paul Taylor electric eco-kettle, Axis (1996), manufactured by Form Design and MEC-Kambrook
Marc Newson chair, Cone (1986)
Josette Orsto and Osmond Kantilla textile length, Kurlama (1994), printed at Tiwi Designs
Hekki Orvola bowl, Kadinaali (1995), made by Helena Murto, Arabia Ceramic Factory
Nora Petyarre textile length of Australian bush designs (1995), manufactured by Utopia Awley Batik
Eddie Puruntatameri three plates, Rijinga (sugar glider) (1995)
Lena Pwerle textile length of Australian bush designs (1995), manufactured by Utopia Awley Batik
Nancy Henry Ripigingimpi textile length, Jilamara (1991), manufactured by Jilamara Arts and Crafts
Paddy Henry Ripigingimpi and Ray Young textile length, Yilinginga (1996), printed at Tiwi Designs
Victa lawnmower, Mulch or Catch (1996), manufactured by Victa
Charles Wilson swivel chair (1993), manufactured by Woodmark International

AUSTRIA
Austrian Museum of Applied Arts, Vienna

Henry P. Glass folding chair, Cricket (1977), manufactured by Brown Jordan Co.

CANADA
Musée des Arts Décoratifs de Montréal

Andrea Branzi lamp, Wireless (1996)
Andrea Branzi bookshelf, Wireless (1996)
Joe Colombo, Multi-Chair (1970), manufactured by Sormani SpA
Tony Cordero lamp, Ecate (1990)
Morison S. Cousins vase, Flower Arranger (1996), manufactured by Tupperware Corporation
Bernhard Dessecker ceiling lamp, Lampeduso (c. 1994)
Height and Guille desk set (c. 1980)
Burt Long fabric, Home Sweet Home (c. 1990)
Ingo Maurer and Team table lamp, Los Minimales Uno (c. 1994)
Alberto Meda and Paolo Rizzatto wall lamp, Lola (1987)
Alessandro Mendini fabric, Museum Market (1993)
Guido A. Niest oil lamp, David (1988)
Jorge Pensi armchair, Toledo (1988)
Charles Pollack chair, Executive Armless Chair (1965)
Franco Raggi suspension lamp, Velo (1987)
Ettore Sottsass vase, Mizar (1982)
Masanori Umeda desk set, Yantra (c. 1995)
Robert Venturi fabric, Large Equal (c. 1990)
Bashir Zivari computer table, Kin-der-link (1996)

DENMARK
The Danish Museum of Decorative Art, Copenhagen

Jacob Berg chair (1996)
Thomas Dickson funnel, Calla (1996)
Dorte Østergaard Jacobsen printed fabric (1990s)
Jacob Jensen computer screen filter with stereo speakers (1990s)
Ole Jensen washing up bowl (1996)
Ole Jensen strainer (1995)
Ross Lovegrove chair, Crop (1996)
Ross Lovegrove themos (1992)
Ross Lovegrove chair, Figure of 8 (1993)
Vibeke Riisberg printed fabric (1990–92)
Vibeke Rohland printed fabric, Sunshine in Transit (1990)
Troels Grum Schwensen chair (1990s)

FRANCE
Musée des Art Décoratifs, Paris

Sylvain Dubuisson one-off desk (1992)
Oscar Tusquets table service, Victoria (1990), manufactured by Follies Driade

GERMANY
Kunstmuseum Düsseldorf im Ehrenhof

Alexander Begge child's chair, Casalino (1970), manufactured by Casala Werke
Sergio Calatroni vase (1996)
A. & P. Castiglioni radio phono combination, RR 126-FO-ST (1965), manufactured by Brionvega
Elizabeth Garouste and Mattia Bonetti carafe, Trapapani (1989), manufactured by Daum
J. Greubel washing drier (1974), manufactured by Braun
Marcello Panza vase, Basilio (1996), manufactured by Pino Signoretto for Coll Bisanzio – Eva Maria Melchers
Giancarlo Piretti chair, manufactured by Castelli
William Sawaya vase, Muranese (1994), manufactured by Sawaya & Moroni
Tobia Scarpa table lamp, Jucker 147 (1963), manufactured by Flos
Borek Sípek vases, Amelia, Marcel and Isotta (1992), manufactured by Driade
Ettore Sottass bowl, Aldebaran (1983), manufactured by Memphis
Philippe Starck vase, Gilbert (1992), manufactured by Driade
Stiletto light, Pflanzlicht (1996), manufactured by Koziol
Matteo Thun glass goblet (1996), manufactured by F.X. Nachtmann
Herbert Jakob Weinand vase, Maskaron Nero (1991), manufactured by Memphis
Weltron radio, Model 2001 (1970)
Yokohama Plant Victor Company television, 3240 GM (1970)
Marco Zanini vase, Rigel (1991), manufactured by Memphis

Vitra Design Museum, Weil am Rhein

Emilio Ambasz and Giancarlo Piretti office chair, Vertebra
Carlo Bartoli armchair Breeze
Riccardo Blumer, Laleggera
Achille Castiglioni lamp, Lampadina
Joe Colombo desk lamp, Topo
Joe Colombo, Multi-Chair (1970), manufactured by Sormani SpA
Joe Colombo table, Poker (1968), manufactured by Zanotta
Michele de Lucchi chair and table, First
Sir Norman Foster Nomos base prototypes
Peter Ghyczy chairs, Gardenegg
Marc Newson table, Event Horizon
Marc Newon chair, Orgone
Frank O'Gehry standing light fixture
Verner Panton armchair, 1-2-3
Pentagon Documenta chair d8
Studio 65, Attica
Marcel Wanders Knotted Chair
Norbert Wangen folding chair, Attila
Robert Wilson Small Stalin Chairs
Robert Wilson Bamboo Chair No.1

JAPAN
International Design Center NAGOYA, Inc., Nagoya

Pierangelo Caramia teapot, Penguin (1993), manufactured by Alessi SpA
Terje Ekstrøm chair, Ekstrøm, manufactured by Stokke
Michael Graves kettle, 9093 (1985–92), manufactured by Alessi SpA
Arne Jacobsen coffee pot and serving tray, Cylinda-Line (1967), manufactured by Stelton
King Kong espresso coffee maker, Mix Italia (1993), manufactured by Alessi SpA
Joanna Lyle kitchen box, Ovo (1994), manufactured by Alessi SpA
Erik Magnussen vacuum jug and serving tray, ABS-Line (1977), manufactured by Stelton
Peter Opsvik chairs, Tripp Trapp, Sitti, Variable Balance, Multi Balance, manufactured by Stokke
Produkt Entwicklung Roericht chair, Stitz manufactured by Wilkhahn
Aldo Rossi, La Cupola (1988–89), manufactured by Alessi SpA
Aldo Rossi press filter coffee maker, 9094 (1986), manufactured by Alessi SpA
Richard Sapper espresso coffee maker, 9090 (1979–92), manufactured by Alessi SpA
Richard Sapper kettle with melodic whistle, 9091 (1983), manufactured by Alessi SpA
Richard Sapper teapot, Bandung (1990s), manufactured by Alessi SpA
Philippe Starck lemon squeezer, Juicy Salif (1990–91), manufactured by Alessi SpA
Philippe Starck kettle, Hot Bertaa (1990–91), manufactured by Alessi SpA

THE NETHERLANDS
Museum Boymans-van Beuningen, Rotterdam

A collection of Authentics plastic items
Andrea Branzi lamps, Wireless made from a birdcage and bucket (1996)
André Dubreuil chair, Spine (1988), manufactured by Vitra
Kaj Franck funnel-shaped vases (1960), manufactured by Notsjö Nuutajärvi
Konstantin Grcic adjustable computer table, Refolo (1995), manufactured by Atlandide/Aleph
Konstantin Grcic chair, Start (1994)
Mag instrument various Mag-lite torches (1996)
Enzo Mari vases, Ecolo (1996), manufactured by Alessi SpA
Floris Meydam crystal vase (1961), manufactured by Koninklijke Glasfabriek
Floris Meydam crystal bowl, manufactured by Koninklijke Glasfabriek
A collection of aluminium Muji objects
Sven Palmquist bowl, Fuga (1960), manufactured by Orrefors
Jan van der Vaart crystal vase, manufactured by Koninklijke Glasfabriek
Sybren Valkema crystal vases (1961), manufactured by Koninklijke Glasfabriek
Marcel Wanders Knotted Chair (1996), prototype

Stedelijk Museum, Amsterdam

David Bade set of plates (1996)
Myranda Brugge vase KS (1981)
Anna Carlgren water-bottle and glass (1995)
Nanna Ditzel bench for two (1989)
Nanna Ditzel table for bench for two (1989)
Nanna Ditzel chair, Trinidad (1993)
Piet Hein Eek chair (1995)
Piet Hein Eek chair (1995)
Piet Hein Eek table (1995)
Piet Hein Eek cupboard, Mono (1994)
Herman Hermsen spot, Torch ST (1982)
R. J. Kokke easy chair (1987)
R. J. Kokke chair (1984)
R. J. Kokke bench (1993)
R. J. Kokke prototype stool TC (1989)
Paul Schudel clock, Axis AK (1991)
Paul Schudel clock, DK (1980)
Henk Stallinga chair (1992)
Henk Stallinga, Blisterlamp (1993)
J. Tresserra desk (1996)
Aldo van den Nieuwelaar lamp, TC 5-85 (1969)
Aldo van den Nieuwelaar prototype cupboard, Amsterdammer (1973)
Hava Zeriker carpet, Slate II (1996)

NORWAY
The Oslo Museum of Applied Art

DDL chair, Blow (1967), manufactured by Zanotta
Brita Flander trays (1996), manufactured by Hackman
Enzo Mari vases made from dishwasher bottles, Ecola (1996), manufactured by Alessi SpA
Gaetano Pesce plastic vase (1995), manufactured by Florian

SWEDEN
Nationalmuseum, Stockholm

Matz Borgström glass service, Matz (1991), manufactured by Lindshammars Glasbruk AB
Nilla Eneroth holder, Januari (1996), manufactured by Hans Lundgren Smide
Brita Flander lamp, Lupti (1993), manufactured by Skanno
Angelica Gustafsson carpet, Klorofyll (1996), manufactured by Hitex Handtuft Svängsta
Ann-Kristin Holmqvist chair, Magistern (1996), manufactured by Trio Snickeri AB
Pia Kristoffersson table pad, Hot (1996), manufactured by Östen Kristiansson AB
Paolo Lomazzi chair, Blow (1967), manufactured by Zanotta SpA
Eva Lilja Löwenhielm mirror with frame, + (1996), manufactured by Östen Kristiansson AB
Cajsa Lund vase, Polo (1996), manufactured by Reijmyre Glasbruk
Hannah Paradis lamp, Anemone Nemorosa (1996), manufactured by Örsjö Industri AB
Caroline Ramberg stacking tables, Satsbord 1 2 3 (1996), manufactured by Skåne Fagerhults Snickeri
Karin Steen candlestick, Magnet (1996), manufactured by Lars Nyström Industri AB
Johan Svensson lamp, Molly (1996), manufactured by Örsjo Industri AB
Barbro Wesslander stool, Krakel (1996), manufactured by Östen Kristiansson AB

Röhsska Museet, Gothenburg

Domestic Design
Monica Backström bowl and candle holder (1967), manufactured by Boda Glassworks
Brita Flander Storm bowl, Hey-Ho glasses, Seven Brothers and Women-filigree goblets (1990s), manufactured by Marimekko
Birger Haglund candle holder (1994)
Torun Bülow Hübe, spoon and bowl (1992/96)
Jan Johansson bowl, Cascade (1996), manufactured by Orrefors
Margon Lindberg bowl (1996)
Åsa Lindström goblets (1996)
Mårten Medebo bowl with lid (1996)
Anne Nilsson vase (1996)
Signe Persson-Melin dinner services (1970–90), manufactured by Boda Nova
Signe Persson-Melin teapot, Kinesen (1980s), manufactured by Röhrstrand Porcelain
Signe Persson-Melin wine glasses, Ruben (1967), Falstaff (1972), Signum (1994), manufactured by Boda Glassworks
Matti Rytkönen Schnapps and Martini glasses, Wolfie (1994), manufactured by Orrefors
Per B. Sundberg vase, Move (1996), three bowls, Lola (1996), manufactured by Orrefors

Tableware
Various pieces of tableware designed by Wilke Adolfsson, Lena Bergström, Karin Björquist, Gunnar Cyrén, Ulla Forsell, Helena Gibson, Margareta Hennix, Gunilla Kihlgren, Markku Kosonen, Helene Krantz, Magnus Löfgren, Ursula Munch-Petersen, Signe Persson-Melin, Anne Nilsson, Ingegerd Råman, Gunnel Sahlin, Sofia Uddén, Ann Wåhlström, Göran Wärff (1970–90), either one-offs or manufactured by Royal Copenhagen, IKEA, Kosta, Skruf Glass Studio, Hackman-Rörstrand, Orrefors
Enzo Mari 1 demonstration box with four vases (1992–95), manufactured by Alessi SpA

Furniture
Gunilla Allard armchair, Cinema (1990s), manufactured by Lammhults
Love Arbén chair, Aron (1990s), manufactured by Lammhults
Åke Axelsson museum bench covered in Nobel Linen designed by Ingrid Dessau (1996), manufactured by Klässbol Linen Factory
Johan Bohlin shelf for the floor, Zink (1990s), manufactured by Källemo
Jonas Bohlin armchair, Concrete (1980), manufactured by Källemo
Don Chadwick and Bill Stopf office chair, Aeron (1994), manufactured by Herman Miller
Björn Dahlström arm chair, BD1 (1994)
Konstantin Grcic tables, TomTom and TamTam (1990s)
Simo Heikkilä chair, Etc (1990s), manufactured by ISKO
Thomas Helleberg chair, Kuling Gale (1987), manufactured by Berga Form AB
Johan Hellström shelf, Kubik (1990s), manufactured by Källemo
Niels Hvass anodized aluminium plate chair (1995), manufactured by Källemo

John Kandell stool, Pax; chair, Schablon/Model; shelf, Pilaster (1990s), manufactured by Källemo
Ralph Lindberg chair, Tati (1989), manufactured by Gärdsnäs AB
Mattias Ljunggren chair, Cobra (1990s), manufactured by Källemo
Bruno Mathsson office chair, Milton (1990s), manufactured by Mathsson International
Steen Östergaard moulded plastic chair (1967), manufactured by Norsk Teknisk Fabrikk
Thomas Sandell chair, TS (1995); stools, Wedding Stools (1990s), manufactured by Asplund
Thomas Sandell armchair, Angel (1997), manufactured by Källemo
Mats Theselius copper-plate screen (1990s)
Mats Theselius book case for National Geographic (1990s), manufactured by Källemo

Lighting
Fagerhult AB table lamp, Robot (1990s)
Brita Flander ceiling lamp, Bembölesäck/Bembölebag (1992), manufactured by Skanno
IKEA PS Collection table lamp (1996)
Jonas Rooth chandelier (1990s)
Table lamp, Lucifer (1990s)

Textiles
5 different printed cottons by Group Ten Swedish designers
Irene Agbaje double ikat, Sainte Chapelle (1995–96)
Gunila Axén fabric, Hommage (1993)
Lena Bergström fabric, Komplissérat (1997), manufactured by Ljungbergs textiltryck AB
Birgitta Hahn fabric, Coquille (1993)
Ingela Håkansson-Lamm fabrics, Mecanique (1993), Grill (1996), Loggia (1994)
Anna Holtblad long black dress (1997)
Fujiwo Ishimoto table cloth with napkins, Misteli (1996)
Katja of Sweden wool coat-dress for MMT (1970s)
Calvin Klein blue jeans (1980s)
Jan Klingstedt napkin (1994), manufactured by Horred Linen Factory
Veronica Nygren tapestry, Avanti III (1988)
Jean Patou evening dress, Alba (1970s)
Luisa Spagnoli cocktail dress (1960s)
Pia Wallén woollen blanket, Crux (1992), manufactured by Östergötlands Ullspinneri

Products
Konstantin Grcic wastepaper basket, Square (1994), manufactured by Authentics
Sven Lundh, Kälemo AB and Sören Nilsen bicycle, The Källemo Bike (1995)
Mari Pårup urn/vase, Summer Dress (1996)

SWITZERLAND
Museum für Gestaltung, Zurich

Ines Bösch various fabrics (1990–95), manufactured by Sourire en Soie AG
Jacqueline Boschung and Brigit Coppo various fabrics (1992–96), manufactured by Boscop
Joe Colombo roll-container, Boby (1969), manufactured by Bieffeplast
René Fehr china, Inflation (1993), Expansion (1993), Rezession (1993), Subvention (1994), manufactured by Lengsfeld Rhön Porzellan GmbH
Daniel and Markus Freitag freeway bags, Lassie (1995), Dragnet (1993), Top Cat (1994), 77 Sunsetstrip (1995), Dallas (1995), Knight Rider (1994), Miami Vice (1993), manufactured by Gebr. Freitag Retour
Willi Gläser shelf holder, G-Pat (1995), manufactured by Gläser AG
Willy Guhl game, Willy Guhl Möbelspiel (1948/49), manufactured since 1995 by Vitra Design Museum
Kurt Zimmerli aluminium bottles (1989), manufactured since 1990/92 by Sigg AG

UK
The Design Museum, London

Itera plastic bicycle (mid 1970s), manufactured by Itera
Clive Sinclair microvision television (1977), manufactured by Sinclair
Sony Design Centre radio, Sony Clip-T2 and headphones, Clip-HD2, manufactured by Sony

Acquisitions from Alessi SpA
Alessitronics alarm-radio, Coo-coo (1996)
Achille Castiglioni, Spirale ash tray (1970), Dry Cutlery (1982–85), condiment set (1984–95), fruit bowl and colander (1995)
Luigi Caccia Dominioni, Livio Castiglioni, Pier Giacomo Castiglioni cutlery, Caccia (1938/90)
after Christopher Dresser thermoplastic resin sugar bowl, Christy
Aldo Rossi espresso percolator, La Conica (1982/84), espresso percolator, La Cupola (1988–89)
Richard Sapper espresso percolator (1977–79/92), tea-coffee pot (1982), milk jug (1982), sugar bowl (1982), cream jug (1982), sugar bowl/butter dish (1982), RS01 cutlery (1995)
Ettore Sottsass cutlery, Nuovo Milano (1987–90), thermos flask, Sherazade (1996)
Philippe Starck parmesan cheese grater, Mister Meumeu, teapot, Ti Tang (1992), creamer/sugar bowl, Sui-Mi Tang (1992)
Marco Zanuso cutlery, Duna (1995)

Victoria and Albert Museum, London

Ceramics and Glass
Jeff Banks tableware, Java and Kabul (1996), manufactured by Churchill Tableware Ltd
Joanna Constantinidis porcelain tableware (1996)
Morison S. Cousins vase, Flower Arranger (1996), manufactured by Tupperware Corporation
Edmund de Waal large porcelain bowl (1995)
Edmund de Waal teapot and beaker (1996)
Dunoon Ceramics Ltd bone china and stoneware mugs (1996)
Eve Midwinter coffee pot and bowl, Stonehenge (1971)

Furniture and products
Jane Atfield chair, RCP2 (1994), manufactured by Made of Waste
Bär & Knell chair (1996)
David Colwell stacking chair, C3 (1989), manufactured by Trannon Furniture Ltd (1996)
Andy Davey/Trevor Baylis Freeplay Radio (1996), manufactured by Baygen Power International
Alberto Lievore chair, Rothko (1989–94), manufactured by Indartu
Gillis Lundgren chair (unassembled and assembled), Ölga (1981), manufactured by IKEA

Textiles
Hanging in devored silk viscose velvet
Bentley and Spens hanging, Medieval Pageant (1992)
Bentley and Spens hanging, Fruit in Bowls (1994)
Gillian Little hanging, Peeling Paint (1996)
Carole Waller hanging, Shrine (1996)

USA
Museum of Fine Arts, Boston, Massachusetts

Tom Dixon stool/lamp, Jack (1996)
Gruppo Architetti Urbanisti, Città Nuova table lamp, Nesso (1962), manufactured by Artemide
Vico Magistretti lamp, Telegono (1966), manufactured by Artemide
Vico Magistretti lamp, Dalù (1965), manufactured by Artemide
Memphis necktie (1980s)
Philippe Starck armchair, Richard III (1986), manufactured by Baleri Italia

Brooklyn Museum of Art, New York

Gerald Gulotta flatware, Eros (1988), manufactured by Sasaki
Isabelle Moore, rocking chair, Amoeba (1995)
Ettore Sottsass vase (1980), manufactured by Fontana Arte
Ettore Sottsass bowl (1959), manufactured by Bitossi (1975)
Ettore Sottsass Pierced Basket (1981), manufactured by Alessi SpA
Ettore Sottsass flatware, Nuovo Milano (1987–90), manufactured by Alessi SpA

Chicago Athenaeum, The Museum of Architecture and Design, Chicago, Illinois

Albini and Helg door lever handle, Agata (1965), manufactured by Olivari
Thomas Albrecht shelf system, Clay (1995), manufactured by Atoll Möbelideen GmbH
Rick Althans and John Whiteman television (1996), manufactured by Zenith Electronics Corporation
Ancona 2 housewares, VIA pasta timer, bagel slicer and kitchen baster (1996), manufactured by B. Via International Housewares Inc.
Gino Anselmi door lever handle, Cusio (1973), manufactured by Olivari
Gae Aulenti door lever handle, Otto A (1983), manufactured by Fusital
Jhane Barnes table, Prelude (1996), manufactured by Bernhardt
Jhane Barnes textile, Honeycomb (1996), manufactured by Knoll Textiles
Carlo Bartoli door lever handle, 2010 (1980), manufactured by Confalonieri
Mario Bellini pen, Persona (1990), manufactured by C. Josef Lamy GmbH
Norbert Berghof, Michael A. Landes, Wolfgang Rang wallcovering, Fries Oder Stirb (1992), manufactured by Rasch
Doug Birkholz garden tool, Power Lever Pro Pruner (1996), manufactured by Fiskars Inc.
Donald Booty Jr flashlight, Flash!Pack (1996)
Bose Design Team music system, Lifestyle 20 (1996), manufactured by Bose Corporation
Klaus Botta binding machine, HiTech (1995), manufactured by Ibico AG
Klaus Botta wristwatches, Eos (1996), Ikon Mechanic (1995), Titan 1 (1994), Uno (1994), manufactured by Watchpeople
Helge Brix-Hansen bottle openers, JarKey (1992), TopUp (1994), manufactured by Brix Design A/S
Julian Brown can compactor, Attila (1996), manufactured by Rexite SpA
Julian Brown, vacuum jug La Ola (1997), manufactured by alfi Zitzmann GmbH
Buchin Design Team lavatory faucet, Aquamix (1996), manufactured by AQUA Butzke-Werke AG
Marde Burke digital answering system, 2-9865 (LDT-1) (1996), manufactured by Thomson Consumer Electronics
Busse Design knives, Four Star (1976), sharpener, Twinsharp (1990), kitchen shears, Twin (1983), manufactured by Zwilling J.A. Henckels
Luigi Caramella door lever handles, 400 (1976) and 410 (1988), manufactured by Confalonieri
John Caruso, Josephine Saavedra, Geoff Broussard candleholder/bud vase, Corners (1996), manufactured by Design Ideas Inc.
Anna Castelli Ferrieri cutlery, Segnale (1996), manufactured by Sambonet SpA
Eric Chan, Jeff Miller, Eyal Eliav knife, X2000 X-Acto (1995), manufactured by Hunt Manufacturing
Clodagh and Nancy Giessberger textile, One Plus One (1995), manufactured by DesignTex Inc.
Luigi Colani door lever handle, Colani (1989), manufactured by Mega
Joe Colombo door lever handle, Paracolpa Alfa (1965), manufactured by Olivari
Gabriel Concari garden tools, Softouch (1996), manufactured by Fiskars Inc.
Nanna Ditzel chairs and table, Trinidad (1993), manufactured by Fredericia Stolefabrik A/S
Luigi Dominioni door lever handles, Saint Roman and Monte Carlo (1979), manufactured by Olivari
Mikaela Dörfel tea and dinner set, Gemini (1995), manufactured by Mono
Alessandro Doria vacuum cleaner, Dirt Devil Broom Vac (1995), manufactured by Royal Appliance Mfg Co.
Wolfgang Dufhues children's flatware (1992), manufactured by Mono
Nathalie du Pasquier wallcovering, Placenza (1992), manufactured by Rasch
Maurizio Duranti bottle opener, Attila (1994), fruit squeezer, Spinoza (1994), manufactured by Mepra
Glen Ediger and Gary Israel appliance, Vornado Heat Rest Plus (1994), manufactured by Vornado Air Circulation Systems Inc.
Wolfgang Fabian pen and pencil, Lamy Spirit (1994), Lamy Swift (1990), Lamy Lady (1994) and Lamy White (1982), manufactured by C. Josef Lamy GmbH
Bent Falk housewares, MultiTower (1989), manufactured by Danish Steel House
Bent Falk stove, Morsø 5040 (1995), manufactured by Morsø Jenstøberi A/S
Siggi Fischer wristwatch, Zwo (1996), manufactured by Watchpeople
Nikolaus Frank virtual analog synthesizer, Nord Lead (1995), manufactured by Clavia Digital Musical Instruments AB
Frauenhofer Institute knives, Twinstar (1995), manufactured by Zwilling J. A. Henckels
Jens Fredslund and Erik Mollers Tegnestue lamp, Et Lumière (1988), manufactured by Louis Poulsen
Fritz Frenckler, Klaus Franck, Werner Sauer chair, MODUS (1995), manufactured by Wilkhahn
frogdesign inc. telephone, ClipFone (1996), manufactured by Astralink Technology
frogdesign inc. computer, Acer Aspire (1995), manufactured by Acer America Corporation
frogdesign inc. wall plate, Surf (1993), manufactured by DAL
Gianni Gagliani vacuum jug, Sculptura (1996), manufactured by alfi Zitzmann GmbH
Gai Gherardi and Barbara McReynolds eyeglasses, Power Tool and Ruby (1996), manufactured by La Eyeworks
Ginbande Design (Klaus-Achim Heine, Uwe Fischer) wallcovering, B100 (1992), manufactured by Rasch
Grohe Design Centre basin mixers, Sentosa (1993) and Taron (1994); shower mixer, Grotherm 3000 (1996), kitchen faucet, Ladylux (1995), manufactured by Friedrich Grohe
Group Four Design paint containers, Creative Works (1994), manufactured by Creative Works
Franco Guanzirollli door lever handle 430 (1991), manufactured by Confalonieri
G. Gurioli and F. Scansetti bendable bookends (1996), manufactured by Zelco Industries Inc.
Peter Hartwein dental care, Braun Oral-B Plaque Control Center (1994), manufactured by Braun AG
Gunvor and Niels Jørgen Haugesen chairs, No. 4 (1994), No. 5 (1995), and Haugesen (1988), manufactured by Tranckaer Furniture A/S
Hauser Inc., Electronics Smart Business Card Reader (1995), manufactured by Seiko Instruments USA, Inc.
Piet Hein lamp, Sinuslamp (1995), manufactured by Unilinc
Poul Henningsen lamp, PH5 (1995), manufactured by Louis Poulsen
Henry Dreyfuss Associates, Marine Analog Gauge (1996), manufactured by KYSOR/Medallion
Herbst LaZar Bell Inc. battery pager (1995), manufactured by Motorola Inc.
Herbst LaZar Bell Inc. carpet cleaner, Marathon (1995), manufactured by Breuer/Tornado Corporation
Herbst LaZar Bell Inc. heater, Holmes (1995), manufactured by Holmes Products Corporation
Herbst LaZar Bell Inc. paper shredder, Shredmaster 60S (1995), manufactured by General Binding Corporation
Hiort-Lorenzen and Foersom chair, Donna (1992) manufactured by Erik Jørgensen A/S
Hans Hollein door lever handle, Flos (1986), manufactured by FSB
Geoff Hollington vase, Trumpet (1996), manufactured by Design Ideas Inc.
Geoff Hollington, Max Burton, Jacqueline Wilkinson candleholders, Palette (1996), manufactured by Design Ideas Inc.
Knud Holscher door lever handle, D Line 112 (1972), M-Handle (1989), manufactured by Carl F. Petersen
Soren Holst door lever handle, Swing (1988), manufactured by B. J. Metal
Alfred Homann lamps, Homann Wall (1987), Nyhavn Pendant (1987), manufactured by Louis Poulsen
Hoppe Design Team door lever handle, K 180 VK (1989), manufactured by Hoppe
Isao Hosoe and Alessio Pozzoli table lamp, Heron (1995), manufactured by Luxo Italiana
Human Factors Industrial Design camping lantern, Northstar (1995), manufactured by The Coleman Company Inc.
Arne Jacobsen lamp, Aj Eklipta (1987), manufactured by Louis Poulsen
Jens Moller Jensen lamp, Orbiter Pendant (1987), manufactured by Louis Poulsen
Jørgen Weber Jensen headset, 405 (1995), manufactured by Danacom
Niels Due Jensen pumps, Type CRNE (1993) and Circulator (1995); Jetpaq Water Supply System (1994), manufactured by Grundfos
Carsten Jorgensen coffee grinder, Antigua (1996), manufactured by Bodum AG
Wolf Karnagel cutlery Epoca (1986), manufactured by M. H. Wilkens & Söhne GmbH
Jorgen Kastholm seating, Terminal/Series 7100 (1990), manufactured by Kusch & Co.
Ulla and Martin Kaufmann cutlery, Palladio (1994), manufactured by M. H. Wilkens & Söhne GmbH
Gregory Kay lighting, Twin Rail System (1995), manufactured by Tech Lighting
Miles Keller dishrack, Plato (1996), manufactured by Umbra USA Inc.
Peter Kövari spectacle frames, Synergy (1991), Synergy 2nd Generation (1994), T-Line (1995) and Wires (1995), manufactured by Rodenstock
Rudy Krolopp, Al Nagele, Leon Soren cellular telephone, Star Tac (1996), manufactured by Motorola Inc.
Bill Lasko and Lasko Design Team, Power Toolbox (1995), manufactured by Lasko Metal Products Inc.
Wolfgang Laubersheimer wallcovering, Tapete (1992), manufactured by Rasch
Scot Laughton tables, Tufold (1996), manufactured by Nienkamper
Rainer Lehn clothes pegs, Sharky (1994), manufactured by Koziol
David Lewis music system BeoSound 9000 (1996), manufactured by Bang and Olufsen

Ludwig Littmann coffee grinder, Café Select (1994) and kitchen appliance, Multimix M880, manufactured by Braun AG
Lunar Design multimedia product, Pippin/Atmark (1996), manufactured by Apple Computer for Bandai
Ian MacColl computer, MultiSync Multimedia Monitor (1996), manufactured by NEC Technologies Inc.
Veit Mahlmann bath accessories, Series 440 (1997), manufactured by Hewi
Peter Maly coffee/tea set Cycla (1994), manufactured by M. H. Wilkens & Söhne GmbH
Peter Maly chair 737 (1993), manufactured by Thonet
Attilio Marcolli door lever handle, Desipro (1988), manufactured by Valli and Colombo
Ingo Maurer lamps, Don Quixote (1989), Bibibibi (1982), Ilios (1983), manufactured by Ingo Maurer GmbH
Alessandro Mendini wallcoverings Colonna and Luna (1992), manufactured by Rasch
Mercatali/Pedrizzetti door lever handle, Sfinge (1982), manufactured by Olivari
Theresa Millard and Jim Neiman sink, Vessels (1996), manufactured by Kohler Co.
Reiner Moll speakers, Nu Form 60/90 (1995), manufactured by Nubert Electronics GmbH
Reiner Moll sink, Volano (1995), manufactured by Villeroy & Boch
Bath accessories, Alca (1995), manufactured by Keuco
Piero Gianemilio and Anna Monti door lever handles, Boma (1971) and Lario (1977), manufactured by Olivari
Gerd A. Müller pen and pencil, Lamy 2000 (1966), manufactured by C. Josef Lamy GmbH
Ron Muller and Joseph Kata appliance, Residential Room Air Filtration System (1994), manufactured by Norelco
Nissan Design International children's furniture, Angeles Base Line (1994), manufactured by The Angeles Group
Paul Ocepek television, The Shark (1996), manufactured by Thomson Consumer Electronics
Mads Odgaard kitchen timer (1991), manufactured by Rosti Housewares A/S
Oregon Scientific Inc. alarm clock, The Time Machine (1995), manufactured by Oregon Scientific Inc.
Jean-Michel Oudot wristwatch, Sapiens (1994), manufactured by Watchpeople
Palo Alto Design Group computer, Pilot, The Connected Organizer (1996), manufactured by Palm Computing
Ole Palsby vacuum jugs Fresh Bottle (1995) and Frosted Kugel (1994), manufactured by alfi Zitzmann GmbH
Ole Palsby cookware, Eva-Trio (1990), manufactured by Erik Mangor A/S
David Palterer vases, Glass Product Research (1995–96), manufactured by Sardinia Crystal
Verner Panton wristwatches, Click Clock (1995), Verner Panton (1990), manufactured by Crival
Verner Panton chair, Shogun (1995), manufactured by Erik Jørgensen A/S
Antonio Pasin wagon, Voyager (1996) manufactured by Radio Flyer Inc.
Peter K. Patzak vacuum jug, Nomos (1995), manufactured by alfi Zitzmann GmbH
Stephen Peart personal Earphone (1996), manufactured by Plantronics
Stephen Peart and Peter Schmidt scanner keyboard, PaperPort (1995), manufactured by Visioneer
Jorge Pensi chairs, Capa/Series 4200 (1996); ¡Hola!/Series 2200, manufactured by Kusch & Co.
Phoenix Product Design basin mixer, Arco (1995), manufactured by Hans Grohe GmbH & Co. KG
Phoenix Product Design pen and pencil, Lamy Black and Lamy White (1996), manufactured by C. Josef Lamy GmbH
Louis Poulsen lamp, Columbus (1993), manufactured by Louis Poulsen
Product Genesis Inc. electronics, Fax View 2000 (1995), manufactured by Reflection Technology Inc.
Product Genesis Inc. firesafes (1995), manufactured by BRK Brands/ First Alert
Dieter Rams door lever handle RGS 1 (1986), manufactured by FSB
Karim Rashid tableware, Nambe (1996), manufactured by Nambe Mills Inc.
RKS Design Inc. speakers, JBL Starion IS1 Multimedia Speaker System (1995), manufactured by Harman/JBL
Heinz Röntgen textiles, Basato (1994), Colonna (1994), Lia-Saki (1994), Nubia (1996), Paloma (1996), Stratos (1996), Teso (1994), manufactured by nya nordiska
Michael Schneider cutlery, Tools (1995), manufactured by Mono
Wulf Schneider chairs 290F (1994), S570 (1990) and S320 (1994), manufactured by Thonet
Michael Shields chair and table, Migrations (1996), manufactured by Brayton International
Dieter Sieger lavatory fittings, Belle de Jour (1997), Obina (1994), Tara (1994), Tip-Tap (1996), Meta (1995–96), manufactured by Dornbracht GmbH & Co. KG
Borek Sípek wallcovering Zed (1992), manufactured by Rasch
Smart Design Inc. tea kettle, wooden tools, bathroom squeegee and ice cream scoop, OXO Good Grips (1996), manufactured by OXO International
Smart Design Inc. office equipment, Details Short Cuts (1995) manufactured by Details
Ettore Sottsass wallcoverings, Arabia Felix (1992), Ercolano (1992), manufactured by Rasch
George Sowden wallcovering, Mention (1992), manufactured by Rasch
Philippe Starck chair, Louis XX (1992); footrest, Dr Oola (1994), manufactured by Vitra
Philippe Starck chairs, Miss Trip (1996), Dr Glob (1990) and Miss Global (1991), manufactured by Kartell
Philippe Starck table, Miss Balù (1990); stool, Prince Aha (1996); magazine rack, Claudia Evangelista (1996), manufactured by Kartell
Philippe Starck sink, Starck WashMobil (1990), manufactured by Rapsel SpA
Philippe Starck door hardware series, PS1 (1991), manufactured by FSB
Philippe Starck vacuum jug, Hot Fredo (1996), manufactured by alfi Zitzmann GmbH
Philippe Starck toilet brush, Excalibur (1995), manufactured by Heller Incorporated
Philippe Starck flatware, Objets Pointus (1986), manufactured by Sasaki
Thomas Stender table, Sigma (1994), manufactured by Modulus
Walter Storr cutlery, Angelo (1996), manufactured by M. H. Wilkens & Söhne GmbH
Peter Tasker medical, Drench Gun (1995), manufactured by Simcro Tech
George Teodorescu ITR 100 Toni Transmitter (1996), manufactured by Leybold GmbH
Matteo Thun wallcovering, Early Eighties (1992), manufactured by Rasch
Kurt Thut chair, S250 (1996), manufactured by Thonet
Tools Design CD rack, CD25 (1993), lemon squeezer (1995), tea ball (1996), manufactured by Tommy Larsen A/S
Alan Tye door lever handle, Quaver (1982), manufactured by Allgood
Tye & Holscher door lever handle, Modric (1964), manufactured by Allgood
Roland Ullmann electric shaver, Flex Integral 5550 (1994), manufactured by Braun AG
Mark Van De Loo scanner, Apple Color One 600/27 (1996), manufactured by Apple Computer Inc.
Lella and Massimo Vignelli chair, Rattan Handkerchief (1995), manufactured by Knoll Inc.
Tassilo von Grolman coffee pot, Cafinero (1996); teapot, Teacolor (1996); tea service, Filio (1988–90), manufactured by Mono
Tassilo von Grolman vacuum jug, Lipstick (1989), manufactured by alfi Zitzmann GmbH
Tassilo von Grolman and Alan Fletcher tea caddy, Twinings (1995), manufactured by Rosenthal
Walter Dorwin Teague Associates computer mouse, Microsoft EasyBall (1996), manufactured by Microsoft Corporation
Johan Weernink storage containers, Contura and Top Cone (1987), manufactured by Rosti Housewares A/S
Werksdesign bathroom accessories, Series 485 (1995), Series 475 (1981); door lever handles 101-USA re-design (1996), 111 (1970) and 117 (1987); coat-racks, Caterpillar, Tree and Branch (1993), manufactured by Hewi
Hartmut Wiese door lever handles (1989), manufactured by FSB
Lori Wietzner textile, Jacob's Ladder (1994), manufactured by Larsen
Heinrich Wilke door lever handle, 115 (1972), manufactured by Hewi
Marco Zanuso door lever handle, Due 2 (1983), manufactured by Fusital
Nicole Zeller and David Tisdale cutlery, Mangia! (1994), manufactured by Zelco Industries Inc.
Zwilling Corporate Development shears, Superfection Classic (1995), Twin L (1989), Twin Lissi (1996); knives, Professional "S" (1992); desk set, Twin Office (1994), manufactured by Zwilling J.A. Henckels

The Cooper-Hewitt National Design Museum, Smithsonian Institution, New York

Richard Carbone and Bryan deBlois flashlight, Snakelight Flexible Flashlight (1994), manufactured by Black and Decker Corporation
Morison S. Cousins kitchen timer, On the Dot (1993), manufactured by Tupperware Corporation
Andy Davey and Trevor Bayliss BayGen Freeplay Radio (1996), manufactured by BayGen Power Company Ltd
Wharton Esherick music stand (1962)
Tetsuji Kawamura table lamp, Bonbori (1993), manufactured by AG Industry Co. Ltd
Ross Lovegrove and Stephen Peart ergonomic work station accessories, Surf Collection (1994), manufactured by Knoll
Richard Miles and John Tree padlock (1992), manufactured by Yale Security Products Ltd
George Nakashima side chair, New (1966)
James O'Halloran Radius toothbrush (1991), manufactured by Radius
James O'Halloran Radius toothbrush, SCUBA (1991), manufactured by Radius
OLO Safety scissors and safety carton opener (1996), manufactured by OLO
Burton S. Rubin prototype model for the 'evo.pen' (1988–96)

The Denver Art Museum, Denver, Colorado

Ercole Barovier vase (1961)
Joe Colombo Multi-Chair (1970), manufactured by Sormani SpA
Morison S. Cousins vase, Flower Arranger (1996), manufactured by Tupperware Corporation
Roy Lichtenstein plates (1969)
Pierre Paulin chair, Ribbon (1965)
George Ranalli sidechair (1985–86)
Borek Sípek dinnerware, Guermantes (1992), manufactured by Driade SpA
Borek Sípek dinnerware and soup bowl, Albertine (1988), manufactured by Driade SpA
Borek Sípek centrepiece, Bersotte (1988), manufactured by Driade SpA
Borek Sípek soup tureen, Berry (1988), manufactured by Driade SpA
Borek Sípek flower goblet, No.101 (1988), manufactured by Alterego
Borek Sípek tumbler from the Veno Pro Xenophona series, Rusalka (1983), manufactured by Anthologie Quartett
Borek Sípek, goblets, Stybla (1984), manufactured by Anthologie Quartett
Borek Sípek champagne goblet, Neboj (1987), manufactured by Sawaya and Moroni SpA
Borek Sípek goblets, Enrico I, II, III, IV, V (1988), manufactured by Driade SpA
Borek Sípek centerpiece, Isotta (1991), manufactured by Driade SpA
Borek Sípek vase, Ajeto (1990), manufactured by Petr Novotny
Borek Sípek knife and fork with wooden box, Ares (1992), manufactured by Driade SpA
Borek Sípek cutlery, Alix (1989), manufactured by Driade SpA
Borek Sípek cutlery, Verwandtschaften (1985), manufactured by Anthologie Quartett
Borek Sípek candelabra, Simon (1988), manufactured by Driade SpA
Borek Sípek bowl, Athena (1994), manufactured by Driade SpA
Borek Sípek sofa, Prosim Sni (1987), manufactured by Driade SpA
Borek Sípek armchair, Bambi (1983)
Ettore Sottsass vase, Vaso Grande (1989), manufactured by Daniel Swarovski Corporation AG
Tapio Wirkkala vase (1970), manufactured by Venini SpA

Los Angeles County Museum of Art, Los Angeles, California

Michael Graves vanity unit, Plaza Vanity Suite (1981), manufactured by Memphis

Metropolitan Museum of Art, New York

Joe Colombo glasses, 5 in 1 (1970), manufactured by Progetti after 1990
Sidney Hutter lamp (1987)
Jacqueline I. Lillie set of glass buttons (1995)
Marvin Lipofsky glasses, IGS III Series No. 1 (1988–93), manufactured by Novy Bor
Richard Marquis glass, Blue Boy's Mamie (1995)
Emanuele Pantanella evening bag (1991)
Frantisek Vízner glass bowl (1995)

Museum of Modern Art, New York

Arian Brekveld hanging lamp, Soft Lamps (1995), manufactured by DMD
Achille Castiglioni ashtray, Spiral (1970), manufactured by Alessi SpA
Achille Castiglioni mocha spoon, Dry (1981), manufactured by Alessi SpA
Annelies de Leede bowl (1993), manufactured by Oak
Vincent de Rijk vase, Kom BV (1986), manufactured by Goods
Maurizio Ficcadenti nail varnish container, Infradito (1994), manufactured by Baralan International SpA
Rody Graumans lighting fixture, 85 Lamps (1992), manufactured by DMD
Bent Hedegaard Nobert hook, Springforce (1994), manufactured by Bent Nobert MDD Industrial Design APS
Hoechst Trevira GmbH Spacenet (1993), manufactured by Hoechst Trevira GmbH
Hella Jongerius vase, Soft Vase (1994), manufactured by DMD
Hella Jongerius lamp, Knitted Lamp (1995)
Vico Magistretti table lamp, Eclisse (1966), manufactured by Artemide SpA
Montse Padrós and Carlos Riart coat-rack, Ona (1992), manufactured by Mobles 114
Tejo Remy lamp, Milkbottle (1991), manufactured by DMD
Tejo Remy chest of drawers, You Can't Lay Down Your Memory (1991)
Paolo Rizzatto table lamp, Costanzina (1992), manufactured by Luceplan SpA
Afra and Tobia Scarpa plate (1991), manufactured by San Lorenzo srl
Mary Shand (Lady Stirling) reading stand (1982), manufactured by Aram Designs Ltd
Studio Tetrarc coffee table, Tovaglia (1969), manufactured by Alberto Bazzani & Co. sas
Jos van der Meulen wastepaper basket, Paper Bags (1993), manufactured by Goods
Marcel Wanders, Knotted Chair (1995)

Philadelphia Museum of Art, Pennsylvania

Andrea Anatasio vase, Lou (1993), manufactured by Vetrofond, Casale sul Sile, for Memphis Milan
Michael Graves tea kettle, Whistling Bird (1985), manufactured by Alessi SpA
Arata Isozaki chair, Marilyn (1972), manufactured by Tendo Mokko
Carlo Moretti srl flute and wine glass from the Cartoccio series (1983), manufactured by Carlo Moretti srl
Carlo Moretti srl bottle (1994), manufactured by Carlo Moretti srl
Carlo Moretti srl flute and wine glass from the Asimmetrica series (1986), manufactured by Carlo Moretti srl
Toshimitsu Sasaki child's chair (1980), manufactured by Tendo Mokko
Philippe Starck table lamp, Ara (1988), manufactured by Flos SpA
Philippe Starck stool, W.W. (1990), manufactured by Vitra International
Shigeru Uchida floor lamp (1985), manufactured by Yamagiwa Corporation

Acquisitions/Photographic Credits

The publisher and editors would like to thank the designers and manufacturers who submitted work for inclusion, and the following photographers and copyright holders for the use of their material (page numbers are given in parentheses):

Ole Akhøj (52 top right) — Aldo Ballo (9 top left, right) — Adolf Bereuter (68) — Joachim Bergamin (51 right) —
Svend Berggren (101 right) — Michael Bogomil (211 right) — Santi Caleca (192) — Carlo Cantini (127, 135 right) — Scott Chaney (159) —
Bitetto Chimenti (74) — Patrick Despriet (164 left) — Caren Dissinger (102 centre) — Rick English (12 top right) — Polly Farquharson (89 left) —
Jane Fitzjones (210 left) — Fotocope Studio (88) — Fotostudio Voorhuis (70 top right and bottom right) — Michael Frank (102 left) — Gill Gane (110) —
A. Gfeller (210 centre) — D. Gilgen (204 right) — Sven Ulrich Glage (98, 99 left,193 right, 197 left, 210 top right) — Lars Gundersen (166) —
David Hall (96 left, 97 left) — Grant Hancock (111) — Julian Hawkins (56, 83) — Dietmar Henneka (35) —
J. Koenigsbeck (199 top right and bottom right) — Yveta Kopicová (136 right, 141 left) — Dorte Krogh (156 right, 167, 193 left) —
Hisashi Kudohu (70 left) — Regina Kuhn (208 right) — Ninna Kuismanen (45 centre and right, 55 right) — Onno Kummer (189 centre and right) —
Per Larsson (128) — Serge Libiszewski (9 centre) — Antanas Luksenas (148–9, 150–1) — Franco Manfrotto — Bassano del Grappa (164 right, 169) —
Mr Martiradonna (185 right) — Tuomas Marttila (41, 42) — Ian McKinnell (182 above centre) — Yair Medina (135 left) — Ole Meyer (205 right) —
R. Müller and C. Knoch (58–9, 64) — Brian Nash (152) — Søren Nielsen (36) — Bart Nieuwenhuijs (153) —
Masahiro Okada (181 top left, top and bottom right) — Kostas Pasvantis (117 right) — Marino Ramazzotti (48) — Randy (180 bottom left) —
M. Ribot (79 right, 94 far right) — Ann Richards (154, 156 left) — Markus Richter (194 top left, 196, 198 right) — Jonathan Rose (63 right) —
Ilan Rubin (197 right) — Michele Sala (95 right) — Schnakenburg & Brahl (37, 46 top right and bottom right, 52 left and bottom right, 71 left) —
Gerrit Schreurs (80) — Jan Chr. Schultchen (211 three images left and centre) — Gregor Schuster (140) — Albi Serfaty (89 right) —
Carol Sharpe (134 left, 199 centre top and bottom) — David Simmonds (12 bottom left) — Filip Slapal (26, 126, 129 centre) —
Michael P. Smith (161) — Uwe Spoering (65) — Studio Azzurro (84, 90–1) — Mici Toniolo (206–7) — Marirosa Toscani Ballo (138) —
Jason Tozer (132–3) — Emilio Tremolada (43 right, 45 left, 49 left and centre) — Andrew Tye (39 centre) — Tom Vack (39 right, 73, 99 right) —
Bart Van Leuven (108) — Lisa Charles Watson (155) — Erik Williamson (131) — Martin Wonnacott (202) — David Zanardi (69)

DATE DUE

GAYLORD   PRINTED IN U.S.A